Mediation for Managers

The business agenda at the start of the twenty-first century focuses on working with change and developing people's potential and performance. The *People Skills for Professionals* series brings this leading theme to life with a practical range of personal development and human resource guides for anyone who wants to get the best from their people.

Other titles in the Series

COACHING CLUES
Real Stories, Powerful Solutions
Practical Tools
Marian J. Thier

COACHING FOR PERFORMANCE
GROWing People, Performance and Purpose
Third edition
John Whitmore

LEADING YOUR TEAM
How to Involve and Inspire Teams
Second edition
Andrew Leigh and Michael Maynard

MANAGING TRANSITIONS
Making the Most of Change
Second edition
William Bridges

MEDIATION FOR MANAGERS
Resolving Conflict and Rebuilding
Relationships at Work
John Crawley and Katherine Graham

THE NEW NEGOTIATING EDGE
The Behavioral Approach for
Results and Relationships
Gavin Kennedy

NLP AT WORK
The Difference that makes the
Difference in Business
Second edition
Sue Knight

Mediation for Managers

Resolving Conflict and Rebuilding Relationships at Work

John Crawley &
Katherine Graham

NICHOLAS BREALEY
PUBLISHING
LONDON

For Oliver and Esme (KG)
For Helen, Isabella, and Olivia (JC)
and for all the managers we have trained to mediate
who have taught us so much

First published by
Nicholas Brealey Publishing in 2002
Reprinted in 2005, 2007, 2008

3–5 Spafield Street
Clerkenwell, London
EC1R 4QB, UK
Tel: +44 (0)20 7239 0360
Fax: +44 (0)20 7239 0370

20 Park Plaza, Suite 1115A
Boston
MA 02116 USA
Tel: (888) BREALEY
Fax: (617) 523 3708

www.nicholasbrealey.com
www.conflictmanagementplus.com

ISBN-13: 978-1-85788-315-2

British Library Cataloguing in Publication Data
A catalogue record for this book is available from the British Library.

Printed in Finland by WS Bookwell.

Contents

Preface

Not all managers would make mediators, but mediation skills will help all managers get better. This book will liberate managers from the stress, confusion, and fear associated with managing conflicts and resolving disputes at work.

Once you have tried taking a mediation approach, you will wonder what all your previous anxiety was about. Even when practical resolution is not possible, understanding and communication will improve. The situation is likely to move on and you will feel calmer, more assured, and more able to refocus yourself and others on day-to-day core activities. The future will also be calmer—your dose of mediation will continue working.

Many managers fear that if they do get too involved in other people's interpersonal conflict, as a third party, they will become a magnet for future staff disaffection. Normally this takes the form of people banging on your door expecting you to resolve their conflicts for them, and blaming you if and when you can't. Mediating managers will be able to survive this and understand how to avoid being stained by the angry, toxic behavior that spills out of conflicting colleagues, staff, and customers. They model positive behavior and guide and coax people beyond conflict to a better, more productive place. Mediating managers are beacons of positive energy, but do not encourage dependency or avoidance. They are enablers not judge and jury; catalysts not fixers; encouragers not enforcers.

MEDIATION SKILLS AT MANAGEMENT LEVEL

This book addresses an unmet need. Most managers are not prepared or confident when conflict occurs. A survey of managers[1] suggested that managing conflict (including grievances and disciplinary hearings) was the second most challenging task for managers and HR staff after managing persistent bad performance. Thousands of staff at all levels have fed back to us during training and mediation sessions that they are profoundly disappointed with their managers' attempts to resolve conflict. In addition, over 60 percent of the workplace mediations we have concluded are between a manager and one of, and in some cases all of, their team. In a significant number of others, managers' attempts to deal with the dispute are generally seen as prolonging or exacerbating the conflict. There is a significant skill deficit in the area of dispute resolution at management level.

Most training and writing about mediation is for mediators, but this book focuses advice, case studies, and skills at the management level. Some managers (particularly human resource managers) will regularly be working as mediators. Others will dip into the mediation toolbox occasionally. Whether you are an occasional or regular mediating manager, you will be a valuable commodity and derive a great deal of satisfaction from resolving disputes and rebuilding relationships at work. Used appropriately alongside other dispute-resolution methods, mediation can really turn conflict around and make organizations better as a result.

HOW THE BOOK WORKS

PART I: UNDERSTANDING MEDIATION

This part outlines our view of how conflict in the workplace takes place, and what makes it so destructive and costly. We explain that the modern workplace is extremely prone to conflict and the importance of getting beyond that conflict positively without too much damage. Using a mixture of conflict resolution and mediation theory, short case studies, and checklists we take the reader through an outline of the mediation approach, and introduce some examples of the types of situations in which mediation skills might be useful.

Part II is a do-it-yourself guide to mediating, invaluable for would-be mediating managers or any managers who need to top up their people skills. Using case studies and real-life examples, we map out in detail the structure of mediation, explain the overall dynamic of the process, and take you through the core skills needed at every stage. Each case study has its own particular demands and characteristics and they become incrementally more difficult. The skills mentioned here are universally useful.

PART II: MEDIATION IN ACTION

Part III uses snapshots of difficult situations at work to demonstrate other areas in which mediation skills are useful, including maintaining dialogue under pressure, investigating sensitive situations, and managing oppressive or discriminatory behavior. The final chapter gathers together practical information about developing the mediation approach in an organization. It includes how to assess the impact of conflict on the organization; some of the current models used to set up a mediation provision; guidance for best practice; where to fit mediation into procedures; and ways of monitoring and evaluating mediation.

PART III: DAY-TO-DAY MEDIATION SKILLS

REFERENCE

1 *Tough Going Survey—Conflict, Bullying and Harassment at Work*, Conflict Management Plus, 1999.

Part I
Understanding Mediation

1
The Potential of Mediation

Two managers had suffered a longstanding "personality clash" that had simmered below every meeting, affected their performance and caused poor communication between their respective teams. Most people avoided being with the two of them.

One day Bob was in the accounts department arguing over an invoice, when Jill walked in to argue over the same invoice. The accounts team froze at their terminals; this, surely, would be show time. Bob and Jill turned to face each other and squared up. Jill took a deep breath … and in walked the accounts manager.

"Jill, Bob, you both look like you have a lot to say."

"Well, I certainly do, anyway," replied Jill.

"You could put it like that," added Bob.

"OK," the accounts manager continued, "so would it be helpful if we spent a few minutes each listening to how the other person sees the situation?"

The accounts team sighed with relief. It looked like someone, finally, was going to help Bob and Jill talk through their differences without it turning into the usual drama.

The above is one of many examples of an interpersonal dispute in the workplace in which mediation can help.

DEFINING MEDIATION

Mediation is a process by which an impartial third party assists people in a dispute to explore and understand their differences and, if possible, to settle them. The parties, not the mediator, dictate the terms of any agreement.

For the last 10 years or so mediation has been seen as the preserve of the "professional mediator"—the fully trained expert called in when a crisis is reached; the lawyer who is trying a less adversarial approach; the quasi-counselor who works with people when they reach desperation point. However, external mediators are often brought in too late, by necessity rather than choice. They are parachuted in and depart, often with a dispute resolved but leaving no new skills behind them. Some organizations have even been accused of avoiding their responsibility for dealing with conflict by bringing in an external mediator.[1]

We believe that all managers need mediation skills. Managers who learn how to mediate will be able to manage different demands, personalities, and behaviors, while setting a positive example. When conflicts do occur they will be able to intervene early, prevent disputes in their own team from escalating, resolve them comprehensively, and repair broken relationships. Teams and colleagues will emerge with a greater understanding of one another, with some tips about how to disagree constructively and a different, more realistic level of trust and rapport.

People who have this approach to conflict are hugely valuable to colleagues on a personal and professional level. It also makes sound business sense. Many organizations around the world have already trained managers and in some cases teams of "peer mediators" to offer a service to people at all levels in their working community.

MEDIATION AND OTHER TYPES OF DISPUTE RESOLUTION

Mediation is often confused with arbitration and people are often not clear what its key characteristics are. Table 1 explains how mediation works and Table 2 clarifies the differences between the various types of dispute resolution.

Table 1 Explaining mediation

What happens in mediation	What mediators do	What people get out of mediation
It is a structured, step-by-step process. It is confidential and speedy. There are separate meetings, then a joint session if appropriate. Issues are clarified. Options are created. Win/win solutions are sought.	Remain impartial, don't judge. Listen and help people listen to one another. Help people communicate. Create a safe environment. Manage conflict constructively. Help people think more creatively about solutions.	Agreements. Understanding/information that can improve future relationships. Better communication if future problems occur. Clarification about misunderstandings. Less stress, more confidence.

Table 2 Mediation and other types of dispute resolution

	Negotiation	Mediation	Arbitration	Litigation
Who makes the decisions	The parties.	The parties.	The arbitrator.	The judge.
Who controls the process	The parties.	The mediator: firmly but informally with the parties.	The arbitrator: relatively informally.	The judge: with a high degree of formality.
Role of third parties	N/A	Independent, impartial facilitator.	Independent, impartial expert.	To act as advocates and discredit the opposition.
Direct involvement of the parties	Complete, but on their own terms.	Full participation in deciding on issues, creating, evaluating and agreeing options.	They input issues, ideas and background material, then the arbitrator decides.	Representatives participate on their behalf.
Types of outcomes that emerge	Whatever the parties are prepared to agree to.	Aiming for win/win, mutual acceptance.	Compromise: between what parties want, based on evidence and technical assessment.	Win/lose: based on legal precedent and consideration of evidence.

All the organizations we work with tell us that staff grievances and complaints are steadily increasing and that managers are finding it difficult to cope. Most procedures for responding to conflict—such as grievance, disciplinary, anti-bullying, customer complaint and harassment procedures—involve a combination of formal and informal approaches, with managers heavily involved in both. The informal measures usually suffer from being ill-defined and inconsistently delivered.

Organizations, like managers, need a practical, fast, humane way of processing all this disagreement and distress. Mediation skills, and the use of mediation in a more formal sense, will enhance managers' capacity to defuse and handle grievances as they arise.

Taking the grief out of grievance

THE BENEFITS OF MEDIATING MANAGERS

Not all managers will make good mediators, but the mediation approach will make all managers better. Mentoring, counseling and coaching skills can significantly help individuals to manage difficult situations more effectively. The particular benefit of mediation is that it takes a collective approach rather than an individualistic one. It starts from the premise that everyone involved in a conflict needs to participate in its definition and resolution.

CHECKLIST
THE BENEFITS OF MEDIATION IN THE WORKPLACE

1 *Cutting the cost of conflict*—the stress, illness, and staff loss caused by conflict often affect the bottom line. Managers who take a mediation role will reduce stress, get people back at work, and keep people collaborating, whether they like one another or not.

2 *Diverting conflicts away from costly adversarial procedures*—where mediation is available, more people choose not to go down a formal route involving investigation and adjudication when they have a grievance against a colleague.

3 *Getting working relationships back on line*—using mediation skills you can produce effective practical solutions to complex issues,

---

build understanding and rapport, and refocus people on their core tasks.

4 *Enhancing communication*—resolving conflict through mediation helps people understand one another, what is required of them, and why things may have gone wrong in the past.

5 *Stimulating healthy change and avoiding stagnation*—conflicts are often caused by different responses to change. Some people wish to hold on to the past, others like to walk all over the past and present and race into the future. Mediation helps people express their fears and concerns and focus on what they have in common. It can reduce the terror of the new by encouraging open communication and feedback. If people feel safe enough to talk and express a view, as well as to hear how and why change is happening, they will be less vulnerable to the effects of change and more able to cope with it.

6 *Fostering dignity at work*—issues of equality of opportunity often cause a tremendous amount of bad feeling and are difficult to handle. Mediation-style interventions have been used effectively in this area to depersonalize the conflicts, to establish what has been happening and what people want to change. Mediation focuses on the specific behavior associated with prejudice, discrimination, and oppression, and creates a safe environment in which people are able to talk these issues through.

7 *Improving understanding of how to prevent costly conflict*—whereas many conflicts previously took on a personal aspect, the process of resolution by mediation also looks at underlying causes, such as organizational difficulties, blurred role definition, or inadequate working practices.

8 *Enhancing people's handling of their own disputes*—contact with less adversarial methods of dispute processing will help individuals to change the way they deal with disputes. People who sample the mediation approach are given a different model to work with. They also rehearse the skills needed to resolve conflict effectively with the mediator, at each stage of the process. People have to listen to get something out of mediation and once you are into the listening habit, there is little reason to close your ears.

INTERACTIVE MEDIATION

There are a number of approaches to mediation and some different interpretations of the mediator's role. Mediators differ in three main areas and it is useful to discuss these briefly so that our own approach—which we call interactive mediation, explained in more detail below—is clear and put in context.

Problem-solving mediators tend to be active in suggesting and evaluating options. The reasoning behind this is that mediators are generally experienced in dispute settlement, they can think outside the parties' limits and bring their own experience and knowledge to bear. Our fear is that this method leaves the door open for mediator power plays, such as premature closing on issues that become difficult, and a lack of ownership from the parties. Within the workplace it also affirms parties' feelings of powerlessness and dependency on "expert" help.

Who develops options and forms decisions?

Interactive mediators fully involve the parties in generating, evaluating, and closing on the issues. This may involve more work, but it leads to improved self-image, as people are brought forward at their own pace, and greater ownership of solutions that are agreed, as they have been reached voluntarily by the parties themselves.

Interactive mediation is a way of working that allows problem solving to happen, but even if no tangible movement on practical issues is achieved, the parties are often able to move on in other ways—in their mutual understanding, approach to future communication, or the way they accept inevitably difficult outcomes. These latter benefits are more important than practical solutions, and often more significant in terms of future relationships, than the quick fix or imposed solutions that a purely problem-solving approach can achieve.

Are mediators there to solve problems or resolve conflict?

When you ask mediators about dress codes, styles of address, and the set-up of rooms for mediation, you touch on a whole range of values associated with people's perception of formality, accessibility, safety, and consistency. Some mediators present themselves and the process as a "cosy chat," others see mediation as more akin to business consultancy.

What degree of formality is appropriate?

We believe that mediators need to be aware of everyone's need for comfort, respect, and independence, and should pitch their degree of formality at the appropriate level. Openness to feedback and research about cultural appropriateness can really help create a structured, safe process without excessive formality.

THE KEY INGREDIENTS OF INTERACTIVE MEDIATION

The overarching term we have adopted to describe our approach is **interactive mediation**. We feel this approach is best suited to the mediation of interpersonal disputes in the workplace. It can also adapt well to other areas such as customer complaints, employment disputes, grievances, and allegations of bullying and harassment, and in this book we encourage you to consider when and how to do this.

Interactive mediation has four main ingredients, outlined in Figure 1, that together help people to feel actualized, having their feelings accepted without judgment.

Figure 1 The key ingredients of interactive mediation

Mediating managers believe that it is possible to maintain a positive dialogue under pressure and do not revert to quick fixes or pressure tactics. They are eternal optimists who seek forward movement until it is clearly not possible. Mediating managers focus on settling disputes, not prolonging or avoiding them. They do this by keeping a positive tone in the face of adversity, giving direction when people seem to be stuck or lost, and remaining solid and dependable when other people start to lose track, panic, or become distressed. This is no easy task but, when achieved, it can transform people's approach to current and future conflict.

Thinking positively about conflict

Many negative conflicts are failures of process. Sometimes no one agrees or sets clear groundrules such as confidentiality or how decisions are made. People do things out of sequence; for example they discuss solutions before mutually defining problems. They do not invest enough time or energy to enable a realistic, workable, mutually agreeable solution to be reached.

A step-by-step process with its own groundrules and structure

In contrast, interactive mediation has clear groundrules about behavior, confidentiality, and equal participation, and its focus is on seeking win/win outcomes. It also has a clear structure, designed to draw the parties into joint working after having first created a safe, constructive environment. As the mediation process unfolds the mediator coaches and coaxes the parties, building their skills and confidence, until they can frame ways forward and commit themselves to agreements. The journey is well signposted and the mediator encourages maximum participation.

Mediating managers know the importance of process whether they are working formally or informally. In the most *formal* setting managers act as mediators as part of an internal mediators' network, as a company's in-house mediator, or as a complaint handler. Their role will have been clearly defined before they start and the parties will know they are in dispute resolution, for example as part of a grievance or complaints procedure, and will probably have received written information about the process before they start.

Informal mediation can happen spontaneously when a manager interrupts two colleagues arguing in a corridor, or when one person comes to complain about another and the manager thinks, "I could really do with getting these two together—fast." In this setting groundrules and structure are still important. The process provides the safety net that allows people to make the moves they need to resolve disputes, both formally and informally.

A set of skills that help people manage conflict constructively

Negative conflict-resolution skills are easy to pick up. Many television shows depict negative conflict, with acrid comments, smart maneuvers, and half-truths paraded with a high moral tone. It is easy to become a conflict voyeur, watching with a mixture of fascination and disdain. There is a high level of energy in such conflict and it may be tempting for people to mimic aggression, manipulation, or avoidance.

Mediating managers learn other skills and use them regularly. They first need to manage how they feel about other people's behavior, reining in their own tendency to judge. Then they need to deploy a completely different set of behaviors, such as reflective listening, win/win problem solving, impartiality, conversation management, option generation, and encouraging closure. These skills help managers handle conflict and resolve disputes, and are useful in a wide variety of other settings.

Actualizing the parties' experiences

People in conflict are not necessarily functioning at their best emotionally. The strong feelings of anger or frustration, despair or guilt that they experience mean that they are often unable to move forward without help. Interactive mediation recognizes their feelings and gives them a chance to feel actualized: seen and accepted without judgment. This allows them to start moving forward and has the potential for transformation. People who felt stuck in opposition can now experience themselves as having the ability to resolve their own conflicts. They start to say and hear what they need to, without falling apart or becoming a victim. Gradually the way they see the other party alters: The other person becomes more "human," less someone who is "all in the wrong." Interactive mediators exercise appropriate control without blame. They offer a safe process, tailored to the parties involved. People often emerge feeling better about themselves.

APPLICATIONS OF MEDIATION

Commercial and publicly funded organizations across the world have used mediation in the workplace for contract disputes, disagreements about customer complaints, insurance and compensation claims, and large-scale disputes about pay and conditions, planning and development. Many environmental organizations use a mediation-style approach to planning, resolving environmental disputes, and more effective "stakeholder dialogue" (see Chapter 9, Using mediation for group disputes).

Mediation is also well established in the international arena and has had many notable successes. Neighbors; family members who are separating or divorcing and disputing over the children, property, assets, and debts; children in playground fights; members of different faiths—these are all groups who for many years have called in mediators to help them sort out their differences constructively.

There are very few famous mediators, as they often work confidentially and almost invisibly. Mediating managers using the skills outlined in this book will be a significant addition to this growing movement.

REFERENCE

1   Bennion, Y & Rogers, A (2001) *Courts of Compromises? Routes to Resolving Disputes*, Industrial Society, London.

2
The Cost and Value of Conflict

Two partners in a medical practice recently went to court in the UK to resolve a dispute. The judge instructed them to build a wall down the center of their office and continue to exist in their separate worlds. They had already assembled a substantial, impenetrable barrier in their minds, so why not reproduce it in bricks and mortar? This permanent physical barrier would in theory limit the continuing damage. For two people who had apparently started off as efficient colleagues, this judgment was a final testimony to the acrimonious impact of their dispute.

Conflicts at work are often like this. They build walls between people who are supposed to be working together. Without appropriate attention a dispute can kill a relationship or infect a whole team. People who should be turning toward one another turn away.

Over the last 10 years, our company, Conflict Management Plus, has seen individuals, teams, and whole organizations pulled apart by conflict, largely due to their inability to act at all, or to a series of knee-jerk reactions that make the conflict worse. Unresolved conflict has a high cost. Like pain in the human body, conflict at work is a sign that something needs attention. Managers often find themselves in the middle of someone else's conflict, which frequently gets worse if left unattended. With workplace conflict and the stress, hurt, and pain that people are causing one another, inaction is inexcusable.

CHOICES FOR MANAGERS

So what choices do you have as a manager when conflict occurs? Most of us select from the four broad strategies available to those in conflict: fight, submit, flee, or freeze (see Table 3). Each strategy involves behavior that is usually driven by habit, an assessment of risk, and a desire for familiar outcomes. We develop these patterns because they help maintain our self-image.

Table 3 Strategies available to people in conflict

Strategy	People can:	By:
Fight	*Contend: The bullying manager* Try to impose their preferred solution on the other party.	Insisting. Blaming. Criticizing. Accusing. Shouting. Using direct and indirect force.
Submit	*Yield: The passive manager* Lower aspirations and settle for less than they would have liked.	Giving in. Giving up. Agreeing just to end the conflict. Surrendering to what the other party wants.
Flee	*Withdraw: The absent manager* Choose to leave the scene of the conflict.	Ceasing to talk. Leaving physically, cognitively, and/or emotionally. Changing the topic.
Freeze	*Choose inaction: The weak manager* Do nothing or wait for the other party's next move.	Waiting. Doing nothing. Allowing pressure to build up.

Under what circumstances would you adopt these strategies? How might you react as a mediating manager if you encountered these strategies from or between the parties?

CONFLICT MANAGEMENT STYLES

Managers develop conflict management styles that affect the way conflict is perceived and handled. These styles—which include the avoider, the controller, the accommodator, and the collaborator—are comforting and are resistant to change, as they are influenced by an individual's concept of the importance of personal goals and relationships with others.

AVOIDER

"I didn't book a meeting room because I didn't know whether you wanted me to."

Avoiders see conflict as something to be feared, and often feel frustrated and hopeless when they cannot achieve their goals. During conflict they frequently give up their personal goals and cannot maintain relationships. They stay away from the issues over which the conflict is taking place and from the people they are in conflict with. For avoiders it is easier to withdraw (physically and psychologically) from a conflict, internal or external, than to face it.

CONTROLLER

"I've booked the meeting room next to my office—I'm sure you can find a place to park nearby."

Controllers pursue their own goals at the expense of others, because relationships are of minor importance to them. They assume that conflicts are settled by one side winning and the other losing, and that they achieve a higher status by winning. Losing gives them a sense of weakness, inadequacy, and failure. They try to win by using power over others—attacking, overpowering, overwhelming, and intimidating—and will defend their position, either because they believe it is the only way forward or simply to win.

ACCOMMODATOR

"I'll come to your office—I'm sure there's a place I can park somewhere."

This conflict management style originates from a strong need to maintain relationships. When conflict happens accommodators do not consider that their own goals are important. They want to be accepted and liked by others. They think that conflicts should be resolved quickly to create harmony, and believe that people cannot discuss conflicts without damaging relationships. They are afraid that if the conflict continues someone will get hurt and this will ruin the relationship. They give up their goals to preserve the relationship.

"What's important for me is limiting my time away from my desk and having a productive meeting—what is important to you, would you say?"

Collaborators value highly not only their own goals but also relationships. They view a conflict as a problem to be solved and a way for people to become more aware of one another's needs. They are good at seeing other people's point of view but do not forget their own goals. They are sometimes not satisfied until solutions are found and tensions and negative feelings have been resolved.

COLLABORATOR

KEY LEARNING POINTS

When using a mediation-style approach to disputes, it can be very useful to recognize the way you respond to conflict, given certain conditions, and to think whether or not your conflict management style is getting you the right outcomes or enabling you to resolve conflict most effectively. You need to:

- Recognize your own patterns of behavior and under what circumstance you might adopt a particular conflict management style.
- Understand how this might influence your management practice.
- Know what alternative strategies are available.
- Develop a variety of skills so that you can adapt the way you respond to conflict.
- Match your strategy to the situation.

WHY IS CONFLICT SO RAMPANT AT WORK?

You might expect that colleagues in an organization would tend to pull together and work as a team. Most managers see themselves as struggling to do a difficult job, juggling many different professional and personal demands, with all too little acknowledgment of their skills and the pivotal role they play. Some managers cope by taking a strong line. There is a fine distinction between managers taking a strong line and bullying. Some organizations take great pride in having strong management—including bullying—and this can be part of a company culture that short-sightedly emphasizes high levels of performance and productivity and ignores supporting staff.

Wright and Smye[1] identify three kinds of organizational culture that lead to high levels of stress and visible or hidden conflict, something they call "organizational abuse":

- ■ Extremely competitive win/lose cultures in which people strive against their colleagues rather than with them.
- ■ Manager-blaming cultures in which people are frightened to step out of line.
- ■ Sacrifice and overwork cultures that involve people putting their jobs and their work above their personal wellbeing, to the extent that they become ill.

A British CIPD (Chartered Institute of Personnel and Development) survey of over 1,000 workers found that one in eight reported bullying at work. The majority were being bullied by more senior staff, including chief executives. The authors comment: "A disturbing number of senior executives are abusing their power by condoning others' bullying."[2] Over half of those in the survey who had experienced bullying reported that it was commonplace in their organization.

Another study of 5,300 employees in Britain by UMIST discovered that 75 per cent of all people who feel they have been bullied say that the perpetrator was their manager. Those who reported experiencing bullying, or witnessed it, suffered poor health, lack of motivation, and low productivity compared to those who were not bullied.[3]

If we are to reduce the amount of conflict at work, we need to change the perception and behavior of managers, especially senior managers. Developing mediation skills is an effective and non-threatening way of enabling managers to manage well, without recourse to behaviors that are or condone bullying.

Managers are already under pressure to perform well, even in changing and increasingly difficult circumstances. We have identified several key changes in the workplace that are

Key changes in the workplace that increase the potential for conflict currently affecting managers and resulting in increased conflict at work:

■ **A shift toward empowering management**—managers are no longer expected to be passive observers or to take over when their own staff's skills need a boost. They are encouraged to coach and empower people to work effectively together.

■ **People speaking their mind**—employees are encouraged to participate more directly in decision making, to take more responsibility, and, where appropriate, to "manage up." When individuals experience this kind of power for the first time they often clash with other people. Fluid, flat teams also place a heavy emphasis on communication skills. Yet little work is done to show these teams how to communicate when differences are emerging and things are not going smoothly. For some people it is difficult to understand the difference between dialogue and argument. If clashes are not interrupted and resolved early they can create an explosive atmosphere in the team.

■ **"All change"**—change is so rapid that people's lives are shifting almost before they have noticed. When boundaries, cultures, and structures alter this rapidly, people find it difficult to get their needs met and, as a result, conflict emerges. Change excites some and threatens others. The negative elements of change that people regularly refer to on our mediation programs for managers include increased competitiveness between groups; rivalries emerging and the forming of cliques; resistance to new ways of working; driving the pace of change through too fast; the loss of a sense of common goals; feeling undermined and disoriented; and a lack of long-term focus.

■ **Managers and teams becoming more distanced**—restructuring in the private and public sectors and the adoption of a matrix approach to teams sometimes lead to a sense of distance developing between staff and managers. The head of welfare for a government body employing 20,000 people across the UK explained, "Without the exposure to and confidence in one another it is sometimes difficult to raise tough issues from manager to team member or vice versa. These issues are then left until they have become unbearable, and escalate rapidly into grievances or disciplinaries. We really need an early warning system and a set of skills which will enable managers to spot this and respond quickly and effectively."[5]

■ **Value conflicts emerging**—mergers and acquisitions often fail, or are significantly damaged, as a result of clashes of culture and values. There is often a heavy concentration on the mechanics of restructuring and change, but the need to address value differences in action is left unaddressed. Mediating managers are well placed to assist in that positive exchange of values and to prevent differences turning into failures.

■ **Local resolution of grievances**—people are more aware than ever of their right to dignity, equality, and health and safety at work. They raise issues that will not always be comfortable or straightforward to deal with. Problems associated with dignity, equality, and safety are difficult to define and often involve a degree of conflict. Managers will inevitably become more involved in handling and resolving such issues. Local resolution by line managers is proposed as the first step in most modern procedures.

■ **Diversity**—changes in the make-up of the working community (such as a growing proportion of women at work and more cultural diversity) have created fruitful opportunities for managers to harness and develop the range of talent, experience, and ideas available. There is always a risk, however, that differences bring about misunderstandings and that errors of commission and omission emerge. At the most serious end of the scale, discrimination and oppression can occur. All managers, not only diversity staff, need to find ways of avoiding discrimination and responding positively to diversity.

■ **The psychological contract**—in order to attract, motivate, and develop staff, more and more organizations are not only offering favorable terms and conditions of employment but also extended welfare provision, child- and family-friendly working arrangements, and support in moments of personal crisis. This more holistic approach to staff care is seen as strongly influencing and enhancing the psychological contract between employers and employees. In short, if people feel better about themselves and their employer they will be more loyal, more committed, and consequently more productive. Negative conflict undermines this sense of wellbeing. Not all staff and managers are in favor of this new way of working and styles can clash because of differing expectations.

THE COST OF CONFLICT

If some of the above factors apply to your workplace, look out—there will soon be a conflict about. Conflict in the workplace can be extremely costly.

CHECKLIST
THE SEVEN INSIDIOUS COSTS OF CONFLICT

There are seven main ways in which conflict can cost organizations time, money, and human resources:

1 **The cost of formal dispute resolution**—formal grievance procedures, industrial tribunals, or litigation are all expensive, generally slow, and often disastrous to relationships. Justice needs to be done, but the most formal route is often justice at a very high cost.

2 **Decreased individual competence**—people work less effectively when they are in conflict with colleagues. Negative conflicts push people's tolerance to the margins. They are less likely to cope under pressure and to meet their own personal and professional targets. They are also more likely to make significant errors. Managers "stuck in the middle" often become fretful and are less inclined to plan ahead. They remain with what they know and play it safe.

3 **Ineffective working relationships**—over the last 10 years we have met a very wide variety of managers, team leaders, and

workers who are disoriented, distressed, and disconnected from their colleagues by conflict. They have not been working to their own fullest potential, nor have they been working well with others.

4 **Toxic communication**—in prolonged one-to-one disputes the people directly involved communicate badly and find it almost impossible to work together. This spills over to peers and bosses. Assumption and innuendo, gossip and rumor proliferate and people either take sides or stop communicating in an effort to avoid the poison.

5 **Impaired staff and team development**—retention becomes difficult when staff are involved in damaging interpersonal conflicts. Some people exit psychologically or emotionally, others sign off sick or leave, since they can no longer manage. Replacing these people temporarily or permanently is time consuming and costly. Teams experiencing negative conflict often find it extremely difficult to move beyond that frustrating stage when no one is working well, decisions take an age, and people feel as though they are walking through glue.

6 **It's raining feelings**—one party to a conflict said that the workplace had changed from being a "desert of emotion" where nobody spoke about feelings to a highly charged environment where feelings rained in from all directions. People personalize issues and blame is rampant. Every conversation becomes charged with emotion and simple decisions take hours because of the level of argument they provoke. People's negative feelings about themselves and one another undermine morale and output is reduced.

7 **Tarnished image**—conflicts that become public affect customers', clients', and shareholders' trust and take the shine off the organization's reputation.

THE POSITIVE POTENTIAL OF CONFLICT

At the beginning of training courses we encourage people from a wide variety of workplaces to share their negative experiences of conflict at work and they quickly and easily remember the pain and frustration. This has two immediate effects.

First, they realize that the negative experiences stick. Secondly, and more significantly, they appreciate that they are not alone. All the other competent, skilled members of these diverse training groups have also suffered the negative impacts of conflict. This realization often encourages them and helps them to recognize that conflict can in fact be positive.

KEY LEARNING POINTS
COPING WITH NEGATIVE CONFLICT

With regard to negative experiences of conflict it is important to:

- Learn from them.
- Recognize that human conflict is difficult and not be too hard on ourselves if we do not manage it too well.
- Ensure that we are not weighed down by simplistic notions of success or failure.
- View conflict as an opportunity rather than a burden to be borne or a hurdle to be overcome.

GETTING BEYOND CONFLICT TO PERFORMANCE

There is a great deal of energy in conflict. People spend a large amount of their time fueling the fire, seeking allies, talking it over with colleagues at the coffee machine (again, and again, and again). Given the pressures that managers are under, any energy flying around the workplace needs to be garnered and harnessed to good effect, not avoided or squashed. Managing conflict well is not about stopping it or dampening it down. It is about working to turn the energy being put into a negative outcome into a positive outcome instead.

So what potentially positive aspects does conflict offer? When we ask delegates on our training course this question they find it a struggle. Many factors can make it difficult for people to see the positive potential in conflict:

- The weight of previous experiences of negative conflict.
- Lack of confidence in their own skills.
- Lack of confidence in other people's ability to respond constructively to conflict.

■ Fear of conflict.
■ Cultural and social pressures (corporate culture) that encourage negative conflict.

However, eventually delegates are able to come up with suggestions such as those in the following checklist:

CHECKLIST
POTENTIALLY POSITIVE ASPECTS OF CONFLICT

■ Bringing issues into the open.
■ Leading to resolution.
■ Being a driver of change.
■ Building understanding of differences.
■ Dissipating anger.
■ Raising awareness of other people's needs.
■ Creating a focus on common goals.
■ Unifying, bonding, and having a positive impact on team spirit.
■ Leading to healthy dialogue.
■ Motivating people to raise issues and discuss new ideas.
■ Challenging existing inadequacies and shortcomings of systems.
■ Leading to review and reassessment of situations and organizations.

KEY LEARNING POINTS
STAYING POSITIVE ABOUT CONFLICT

In order to hold on to the positive potential of conflict managers will need to:

■ Expand their repertoire of conflict management skills.
■ Pay attention to positive moments and hang on to them like gold.
■ Encourage others to feel more positive about conflict.
■ Learn how to use a mediation-style structured approach designed to resolve conflicts early and fully.

REFERENCES

1 Wright, L & Smye, M (1998) *Corporate Abuse*, Simon & Schuster, London.
2 CIPD survey (1996) London.
3 University of Manchester Institute of Science and Technology (UMIST) survey, Cooper, G & Hoel, H (2000) TUC, London.
4 Irene Murdoch, Inland Revenue Welfare, correspondence in 2001.

3
The Mediation Approach

Human conflict poses a unique challenge: How can we achieve our personal goals and get our own needs met, when those goals and needs appear to be in opposition to someone else's? There may also be a clash of values, beliefs, and behaviors. If we have an ongoing relationship with the other person, for example if they are a colleague or one of our team members, the dilemma becomes even more difficult.

An individual can be represented as in Figure 2.

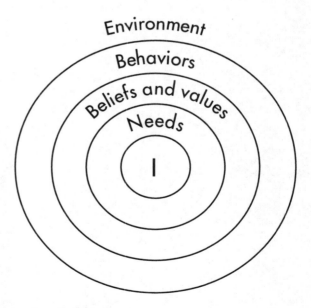

Figure 2 Circles of influence

Philip worked in a pharmaceutical company, was well paid and given responsibility. It was a fantastic job. Yet he found it increasingly hard to go to work with enthusiasm, as he began to doubt the validity of animal experimentation. He became carping and negative and began to underperform. Managers started to view him as difficult. In the end he went through a disciplinary procedure and left.

Philip in the example above is affected at the center of his being. Inside all of us is our self, the heart of who we are and who we strive to become. Some call this our soul. This inner circle is a mixture of what we know, what we know that we don't know, and, most of all, what we don't know that we don't know. For comfort, most of us only recognize and work from the bit of us that we know we know. The rest lies fallow, unless something happens that forces us to consider this area. This internal core is independent from our culture or background, class, age, or gender.

The core

Around this core lie our needs. These include human essentials such as a roof over our head and food, but they also include more relationship needs, identified by many as including the need to be heard, known, and recognized, to be validated, to be loved and to love. All people in all cultures experience these. We often only recognize our needs, or can articulate them, when we feel they are under attack or are not being met. Philip is no longer getting his needs met at work and becomes upset and disoriented.

Needs

Around these needs are our beliefs and values. They stem from our core and from our needs, and are influenced by our culture. Some come from upbringing. We all have certain beliefs and values that spring instantly to mind: "Cover your mouth when you cough," "Being honest is good as long as you don't hurt others," "My private space is my own kingdom—knock before you come in."

Beliefs and values

Some beliefs come from messages from our culture about our apparent role in it. For example, "I don't feel comfortable showing emotion; it doesn't feel manly," or "I like taking care of people, making sure they feel OK. I guess it's part of being female." Others may be the reverse of traditional beliefs and come from the subcultures of which we are members. Some values are hard won from our personal experience. For example, people in the subgroup "mediator" may value openness and believe that talking honestly and hearing others means that almost all differences can be resolved.

A consistent identifier of our personal beliefs and values is that they feel to us to be normal, right, a sign of mental health. Philip's beliefs and values are being challenged on a daily basis at work. He may wish to hide or suppress this but it will be a potential cause of stress.

Behaviors

The next layer, behaviors, is how we actualize our beliefs, values, and needs to the world. Behaviors are often automatic, spontaneous; sometimes we are surprised at our own behaviors. However, they can also be hampered by our internal beliefs and values. Some of us laugh loudly when we hear a joke, but we choose not to laugh at jokes that humiliate others. Or if we do, we feel shame and guilt close behind the laughter. Philip's behaviors are, it seems, detrimental to colleagues, and the clash his work poses to his needs and beliefs is contributing to this.

Environment

The final layer is the environment, the physical space around us. Changes in the environment, such as moving work areas or changing locations, can produce significant increases in conflict as tensions work through the zones to your inner core. Customer care books advise relocating complainants to a private or more neutral environment, precisely because of the effect our environment can have on mood and confidence. The use of color therapy, feng shui, and taking a holiday all spring from this notion.

We behave in different ways according to our environment. For instance, we can be highly effective and articulate in our internal environment (in our thoughts), quite effective at home and with friends, and reach a peak at work, but hopeless when faced with a formal environment such as a large conference room or a police intake area. Largely, however, our environment is made up of *other people's* behaviors.

Congruence and conflict

Internal congruence is achieved where a consistent thread connects all these circles: our behaviors match our values, our needs have a good chance of being met as a result of our behaviors, our values support our "soul." Each stems from, and feeds into, the other parts. We feel psychologically healthy and appear so to others.

Internal conflict arises from a mismatch or dissonance in the circles. Someone who smokes may believe that smoking is highly damaging to health and value their life, though they still smoke. We can be triggered into conventional behaviors that go against some of our values, such as conceding to apparently powerful people when we believe in equality. These and the hundreds of other incongruencies within us result in shaky, inconsistent behaviors and complex feelings.

THE CONFLICT ZONE

Our internal contradictions and tensions are enough of a challenge for many of us. It can be hard going to work and maintaining a professional, competent image—a set of behaviors—when for whatever reason our internal world is fighting against this. Likewise, it can be hard maintaining our internal equilibrium when the external world is fighting our values, not meeting our needs, or criticizing our behaviors. Introduce another person in potential opposition and this is where the conflict zone appears (see Figure 3).

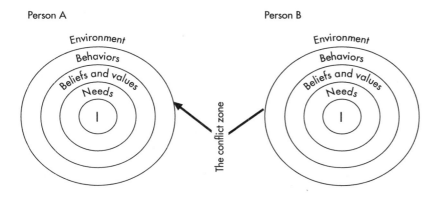

Figure 3 The conflict zone

We can clash at every level: behavior to behavior (primarily the focus in problem-solving mediation), values to values, and so on. "Personality clashes" are our most common experience of the conflict zone. Sometimes we are unaware of or unable to express what our beliefs and needs are, leading to a strong sense of confusion and vulnerability, as well as confusing and inconsistent behavior toward others.

A male manager had a newly appointed female second-in-command. As a good manager should, he supervised her work closely, helped her learn from his experiences, and encouraged her to take further qualifications in her field. He dropped in to her office, propping the door open on his way out to let her know that he was an informal manager and she could relax and open up with him. He believed in her skills and was keen that they should be seen as a solid team. He tried to build her confidence with frequent compliments.

He was therefore amazed when she took out a grievance against him, alleging that he bullied her, overmonitored her work, took credit for her ideas, wouldn't give her real work to do but instead offered her routine, administrative work, implied that she was inadequately qualified for the job, made unwanted personal comments, and was intrusive and disrespectful of her private work space.

Conflicts arise because "other people are not like me." As we saw in the previous section, we all have our own internal beliefs, values, and needs, which we show to the world through a set of behaviors. We register other people's behaviors and instantly fit them into our world view, comparing them to our beliefs and values, assessing the possible needs of that person, and often drawing conclusions about their value, worth, and personality.

First, we overlook the fact that many of us do not work congruently all of the time. Sam, a man who respected women and demonstrated this when in only female company, found himself behaving as "one of the lads" when in a group of men. We hear the loutish comments, see the smirks, and conclude that Sam is either hypocritical or weak. We don't often pause to consider that perhaps he is finding it difficult to behave congruently, that he may be experiencing high levels of stress as a result of his behavior failing to meet his values. Even more rarely do we consider that perhaps our own beliefs and values about consistency of behavior may simply not be the same as his.

Secondly, we don't take into account the effects of our behavior on other people's needs and beliefs. Because our beliefs and values feel to each of us to be so right, we insist on applying them willy-nilly, or argue to prove our rightness and normality. We resent being judged by our behaviors—we know that we are more than our behaviors—yet we are often quite happy to judge and label others by their behaviors.

The conflict zone is the space where, in the absence of further information, we draw the best conclusions we can about the other person's beliefs, values, and needs. He walks into my office without knocking? He is rude and inconsiderate. She talks about me to others? She has no professional integrity.

Third parties are often seen as the arbiters of whose values and behaviors are right and appropriate. People in dispute look to them for this evaluation. Mediators do not fall into this trap, however. The role of the mediator is "to boldly go" into this territory to help the disputants identify what they have interpreted, to enable them to question, clarify, and acknowledge difference, to allow them to connect not only behavior to behavior but value to value. Words like "professional," "respect," and "appropriate" are shorthand for a person's set of beliefs or underlying needs, and a mediator's job is not to judge whose set is better, but to allow clarification and connection. In short, mediators help people interact so that they make more of themselves visible to the other in order that their subsequent responses and beliefs about each other are more reliable and congruent.

CASE STUDY
A MANAGER GETTING OUT OF THE CONFLICT ZONE

Sian was the communications manager for a large UK charity. She had recently appointed James, a designer whose job required frequent contact with production officer Helga. Although Sian recognized that things were not going too well, she had put this down to early teething troubles and left them to sort out their differences. She only realized the strength of feeling between them when three weeks after James's appointment Helga appeared in her office and burst into angry tears.

According to Helga, James was rude, aggressive, and patronizing. He wasn't consulting her on design decisions that had an impact on her production work. When Helga had tried to raise this with James informally, he had accused her of being possessive and a control freak.

Sian knew that her conflict management swung between avoiding conflict and overcontrolling it. She was prone to troubleshooting on the spot, getting the individuals together and laying down the law, or telling people to sort out their mess for themselves. This time, she took a slower but more effective line. She talked to James and heard his point of view. Helga was a poor communicator and worked by the book, she had little understanding of design, and seemed to want everything done her way. He was fed up with feeling constrained and under attack at work and was considering leaving. Although Sian had no mediation training, she had been through mediation herself when separating from her partner, and she recognized that this might be a good approach to help James and Helga sort out a working relationship. The way they had opened up to Sian gave her a clue that she had already established good rapport with both of them. She wanted to try to keep them both on her team without things getting formal.

Sian considered her options and, rather than getting James and Helga together, having a session to clear the air, and then her saying what they were going to do, she decided to take a more mediation-style approach. Having reached the decision not to make judgments and to hold off from her more usual arbitrator role, bringing the two of them together felt to Sian a little like going white-water rafting while blindfold. The atmosphere was tense and stuck, with Helga and James both skirting the issues. Helga had worked with Sian for several years and thought she knew her management style, so was expecting Sian to give an overview of the situation, hear both positions, and make a decision about the way forward. This was the way Sian had previously operated and it was hard for her to hold back, but she reminded herself, and Helga, that she was in "mediator mode" during this meeting.

Sian maintained rapport by subtly echoing the language that each was employing. Helga used feeling expressions, like "It feels unfair that I can't do my job … it's uncomfortable when I try to talk to James," while James used more visual language, such as "It looks like Helga is always out to get me … I can't see any way forward." Sian also maintained rapport with each of them by not judging what they were saying, but reflecting back in neutral terms so they felt heard and accepted by her, at least.

The conversation was getting more heated as Helga and James accused each other of being unprofessional and having no respect. The closer the accusations went to their core values and self-image, the more strongly they defended themselves. Sian could feel herself being drawn into the conflict zone, her breathing was getting lighter, and she had to stop herself from giving voice to the increasingly strong judgmental views forming in her mind. She reminded herself that she was trying to mediate not arbitrate, and decided to put her own values and judgments on hold.

Her preferred personal style was to work quickly and intuitively, but she acknowledged that this behavior could have a potentially high impact on the interactions between the three of them. She realized that she needed to feel in control of what was happening, but gave herself permission to relax that control, and instead to allow the two people with the conflict to decide for themselves what was going on and what the issues were. So she decided to get them to check their assumptions and labeling of behavior.

Sian started by asking Helga and James to each explain what general terms like professional meant to them, and in as practical a way as possible how they saw and experienced concepts like respect and appropriate behaviors. What emerged was more common ground than either had expected, as it became clearer that both were seeking a professional relationship, that both wanted to feel respected and to work confidently with their peers, but that they had different ways of manifesting these values.

Once James and Helga recognized the positive intention behind each other's apparently hostile behavior, they were able to move on and agree rules for their future interactions. Now they knew a little more about each other's beliefs and needs, they were able to meet them accurately.

Sian was pleased with the outcome of the meeting. She had kept things moving forward, and she believed she had helped Helga and James say things that helped clarify their views and cleared the air, precisely because the atmosphere she had created for this meeting was one of not judging but optimism, and expecting her staff to be able to take some responsibility for their working relationships. The whole process, from when Helga had arrived in tears to the closure of the joint meeting, had taken longer than her normal route, but Sian now believed that James and Helga were on a firm footing with each other and wouldn't be reappearing in her office expecting her to resolve any future complaints—the all-too-common outcome of taking a more adjudication-related approach that feeds people's belief that they cannot sort out their conflicts without someone else deciding on right and wrong.

RAPPORT: AT THE HEART OF MEDIATION SKILLS

The key skill that enables mediators to achieve effective communication with others is rapport. Rapport is a state of connectedness, where each person feels that at least part of their values and beliefs is recognized and accepted. Deep rapport, such as exists between friends and partners, signifies that their needs are matched and being met, and that there is some actualization of the inner "I" or core.

The type of rapport needed by mediators is less deep than this and is achieved through a variety of means. A number of these skills are outlined throughout this book. In essence, rapport allows people to communicate openly, as they trust that their world view, values, and behaviors won't be criticized or attacked. Building rapport means aiming to understand what is important to another person.

Rapport is achieved partly through modeling, mirroring, and pacing. This means building a bridge with the other person by using their language, speaking speed and style, and pace of speaking. You should also acknowledge them without blame. Once you have this connection you can lead them, for example inviting them to look at a situation differently or moving away from emotion and toward objectivity. Rapport is also built through achieving and demonstrating empathy, active listening, questioning, silence, and neutral language.

KEY LEARNING POINT
ACKNOWLEDGMENT AND RAPPORT

Sometimes a third party using a mediation-style approach may need to give unwelcome information, or ask people to focus on one area, or ask for a change in behavior. This can put great pressure on the rapport between you and may, if poorly done, feel to the other party like a conflict, to which they may react by withdrawing psychologically or physically, or by attacking.

At such moments remember the three As:

- **Acknowledge feelings**—recognize how they may be or have expressed that they are feeling, in non-judgmental language.
- **Accept their right to feel the way they do**—do not challenge, deny or question their right to their feelings, before moving on to…
- **Action**—e.g., asking them to change focus, or explaining something potentially negative.

TAKING THE BLAME OUT OF INTERACTIONS

One problem facing mediators working in the conflict zone is the impact that the parties' behaviors have on the mediator. As a mediator, you need to ensure that your own contribution to this zone is minimal, that you keep out of it your own beliefs about fairness, professional behavior, what is "right" or "appropriate." Mediators demonstrate a neutral response to behaviors that don't match their own values, and remain impartial when one side appears to have more in common with their needs than the other.

We live in a society that encourages us to make snapshot decisions about people and their worth, based often solely on their visible behaviors. For instance, the popularity of voting people out of a reality TV program on the back of heavily edited footage about them is based on our propensity to judge others.

As managers our role often becomes that of an adjudicator, the person who decides what is appropriate and what not.

The problem in this approach is that we are in effect building an additional wall in the conflict zone, rather than enabling disputants to start dismantling the walls they have erected between themselves. By taking sides and losing neutrality managers shut down communication, lose the potential for disputants to build recognition or to exchange views and feelings before being able to move on. The judgment is there, so moving on is only possible as prescribed within that judgment. The skill of maintaining impartiality and neutrality is outlined in full on pages 79–83.

By encouraging parties to exchange views without blame, mediating managers divert the momentum away from trading labels toward settlement, moving on, and achieving resolutions that all parties can live with.

CASE STUDY
GIVING PEOPLE A CHANCE TO STEP BACK

Lucy and Andrew are senior managers of a small department within a major IT company. Lucy reported to Andrew, but the relationship was an unhappy one and the tensions between them were now affecting the performance of the others in the team. Andrew came to Ivan, the head of HR, to talk through the possibility of taking out formal disciplinary action against Lucy. Ivan, who tended to avoid conflict whenever he could, explained the procedure that Andrew would need to follow. He then took a deep breath and tried something different, by talking with Andrew about the pros and cons of using an informal dispute-resolution process.

Talking it through with Ivan, feeling that he was interested in this situation and didn't just want it off his desk, Andrew was able to acknowledge that he really wanted Lucy "back on board" and some kind of workable relationship established between them. He didn't want to take a formal step, as he realized that the effect on the team could be even more damaging.

Andrew asked Ivan to talk to Lucy, but asked that he didn't disclose what the two men had discussed. Normally Ivan would have avoided situations like this, viewing it as getting too involved and rescuing the situation, which he didn't want to do. But he had agreed with Andrew to try this different approach.

When Ivan met with Lucy, he explained that Andrew had come to him because he would like the situation between them to be improved, and that although there were specific issues Andrew would like to talk through with Lucy, Ivan was not there to discuss these but to check with Lucy how she saw the relationship. Lucy was immediately defensive. If Andrew had something to say why couldn't he come to her direct? If she had done something wrong then Andrew could discipline her, for all she cared. She was extremely angry and seemed quite prepared for a fight with Andrew, and with Ivan too.

Ivan felt like running away. He didn't like the feeling of being attacked and was uncomfortable with Lucy's anger. But he kept himself calm and used the three As to maintain rapport with Lucy: "I hear how strongly you feel about my coming to talk to you like this, and of course I am not here to tell you how you should feel. From where you're sitting this must seem pretty odd. Perhaps you could tell me a little more about why you don't want to talk to me?"

Lucy felt relieved that Ivan hadn't argued with her about her frame of mind and felt more able to trust him, so she disclosed a little more about her experiences with Andrew.

Ivan heard several things that didn't chime with the version he had been given by Andrew, and he was tempted to throw in the towel, go back to Andrew, and report failure. But he realized that this would not be constructive or neutral, because his own behavior would be influenced by his judgment about Lucy's behavior. In addition Lucy made several personal comments about Andrew, including that he was "totally sexist." Ivan felt a strong instinct to challenge this as inappropriate, or to check with her if she felt she was being treated differently because of gender, sensing a sexual harassment case in the offing. But he kept a focus on his goal, which was to give both people a chance to step back and resolve their conflict early and informally rather than fighting to the death. Instead, he continued to ask non-blaming questions and reflect back what Lucy was saying, until he and she were clear what the issues were for her.

At the end of the meeting, Lucy was willing to trust that Ivan would not judge her and she had moved her position away from her early defensiveness. She was willing to meet Andrew to talk things through, as long as Ivan was there to mediate formally, if she and Andrew were unable to resolve matters between themselves.

TAKING THE ADVERSITY OUT OF DIVERSITY

Many organizations have equal opportunities policies and staff expect that anti-harassment guidelines will be implemented and taken seriously by management. However, profound conflict and debilitating unrest are often caused when people find that managers either ignore or indirectly comply with harassment at work. Inadequate managerial responses can reinforce rather than resolve sexual harassment claims. Even when organizations recruit on an effective equal opportunities basis, this may not extend to work practices.[1]

No wonder, then, that organizations are increasingly experiencing accusations of harassment, bullying, and discrimination. Workplaces are changing fast and managers face growing insecurities. We commonly hear managers saying that they are concerned about everything they say and do when directly managing the opposite sex, black and minority ethnic people, or those with disabilities, because they fear being accused of harassment. This creates situations where some managers are afraid to act, some managers over-react, and staff can feel forced by procedures and policies into formal grievances where their preference might have been to resolve difficult situations informally.

The concept of "dignity at work" has reasserted the rights of workers from all backgrounds, cultures, ages, levels of ability, and sexuality to enjoy the right to pursue their work untroubled by bullying, harassment, and persistently oppressive behavior from colleagues and senior staff. This is a welcome reframing of the issue, as it gives all staff a focus on what can be different in the future, as well as what was wrong in the past. Mediation can really help people work together on these difficult issues.

What mediation can offer in conflicts involving equality and diversity issues

For the last 10 years there has been a debate in the UK about the validity of mediation in cases involving equality issues. Some of the early fears were:

- The victim would be obliged to meet with the person who had been harassing or bullying them.
- The victim's rights would somehow be compromised.
- The emotive content of the issue would be difficult to express, hear, and resolve.
- Mediators were not sufficiently well trained or aware of issues associated with oppression to enable effective mediation.

In the workplace, grievance and harassment procedures have been developed that focus on ensuring the following:

- The experience of the victim is taken seriously.
- Steps are taken to pursue cases of harassment and bullying.
- Sanctions are available to deter future harassment and bullying and protect current and potential victims.

What has been missing from many grievance procedures, nevertheless, has been an opportunity to address bullying or harassment early, and to achieve measurable behavioral changes to prevent it recurring or escalating.

Mediation provides an early opportunity to get feelings heard in a way that can move the situation on, and often gives parties an opportunity to resolve conflict constructively, as the focus is on the future and how to make practical changes. By taking a mediation approach, the manager creates a structured, safe environment, which itself creates controlled communication. Power differentials that can often influence situations in which harassment persists are balanced during this type of meeting. The emphasis is on direct, open communication without blame but with acknowledgment of responsibilities, which makes it possible for parties to achieve progress.

For mediation to be successful in cases involving equality issues, managers need to be fully trained in the principles of mediation, the use of mediation skills, and the structured mediation process. They need to be aware of the issues associated with prejudice, discrimination, and oppression so that they can recognize these, and respond neutrally and empathetically. Power and status issues need to be addressed in a constructive way, and the high levels of emotion that go along with issues of harassment and equality need to be managed sensitively and with good control. (See Chapter 8, Mediating a high-conflict situation, and Chapter 11, Responding constructively to the "isms.")

CASE STUDY
WE'RE NOT RACIST BUT...

John, a Catholic working in a largely Protestant team in Northern Ireland, went to his line manager, Libby, to complain about the sectarian comments and taunts he was being subjected to by his team mates. His line manager used open, clarifying questions and neutral reflection to make sure that she and John were clear about the issues and how John felt about what was going on.

It became clear to John that what he wanted was for the comments to stop. He didn't want to make a formal complaint and by and large he was happy working with the group, if only they would realize that their jokes were unwanted. He had not reacted to any of the comments because he felt outnumbered and did not want to seem churlish, but he had now had enough.

Libby agreed that the matter required attention and discussed with John how she would introduce the subject. She asked the team to meet "because she wanted to look at the way they were working together" and "she was unhappy with some of the behaviors she had noticed." She started by saying that with John's permission she would get right to the point. She wanted to look at the issue of sectarian banter in their team. She took some time to establish with the group what groundrules and group norms needed to be agreed, so that everyone could get on with the discussion. John made the first contribution and was quite emotional, but Libby protected his time, stopping interruptions and telling everyone that they would get a chance to respond. Before people did respond, Libby reminded them that it should be the whole team's goal to move the situation forward.

When people got stuck or denied that there were any problems, Libby quickly refocused them. "This is not about who is to blame or what your intention was. We're here to move forward, so what as a team are you going to do about sectarian banter? I know it is part of the fabric of your life."

John suggested that they work out some group and team guidelines. They did this, wrote them on the board for future reference, and both John and the team agreed that a difficult situation had moved forward. He had made his point without being victimized and Libby had maintained a progressive, safe environment. People felt "put on the spot" but not blamed.

KEY QUALITIES OF MEDIATORS

Interactive mediation requires managers to develop a set of skills, and an approach to conflict, that some people may find easier than others. It will be an easier road to travel if you start the journey with some key qualities, as follows:

- **An A-grade listener**—prepared to be patient, attentive, and understanding of what other people say; prepared to assume people are telling the truth; able to silence the internal conversation that many of us have when listening.
- **Non-judgmental and open-minded**—not getting drawn in, offering your opinion, or criticizing even when you might have thought or behaved very differently from the people with whom you are working; able to live with "gray areas," not being driven by a search for the one true version; accepting of people's differences; able to respond constructively to a wide variety of people, ideas, and different ways of thinking.
- **Capable of staying calm**—responding positively and fairly to difficult behavior, staying focused and unfazed, thinking creatively under pressure.
- **Positive under pressure and good at getting the best out of other people**—able to manage other people's frustration and aggression in a constructive way; not taking things personally; remaining relentlessly constructive and realistically optimistic; being a good communicator, able to encourage, prompt, and be persistent when necessary.
- **Aware of issues associated with equality**—showing understanding of prejudice and discrimination, harassment and

bullying; working in a way that demonstrates in a practical manner respect for and acceptance of differences.

■ **Able to maintain confidentiality**—prepared to work without disclosing details of disputes, issues, or behavior before, during, or after contact with clients, and able to resist pressure for inappropriate disclosure from individuals or groups within your organization; respecting the other key principles of confidentiality (see Chapter 4, A map of the process).

■ **Organized**—able to work in a structured way, keeping people informed, managing venues and the small amount of paperwork required.

ENCOURAGING PEOPLE TO MEDIATE

We have often wondered why mediation is so hard to "sell." On the surface it appears like a winning idea. Mediation has the following benefits:

■ It is fast acting.
■ It is private.
■ It treats you like an adult.
■ It leaves you feeling competent and effective.
■ It doesn't close other doors if not satisfied.
■ It takes away the conflict in nine out of ten cases.

Mediation should be irresistible to anyone in the midst of painful, ongoing conflict at work, and yet all kinds of people, for many reasons, frequently resist it.

Reasons for resistance

Resistance to mediation is often rooted in areas such as the following:

■ **Misunderstanding and lack of information**—mediation is still seen as counseling, meditation, and compromise.

■ **Fear of conflict**—many of us were brought up to avoid conflict and to be scared of voicing our needs, or we are afraid of being shouted at or criticized.

■ **Skepticism about results**—we generally view ourselves as competent communicators, so how can something that calls

Table 4 Where mediators hope to guide the parties

Initial behavior	Mediator skills	Final behavior from parties
Defensiveness.	Rapport, listening.	Opening up.
	Impartiality.	Moving from "you" to "I" statements.
	Neutral language.	Acknowledging things could be improved/there is a problem.
	Funnel technique in questioning.	
Aggression.	Defusing.	Stating real issues.
	Empathy.	Focusing on issues.
	Questioning.	Non-blaming language.
	Appropriate control.	
	Assertiveness.	
Inertia.	Probing and prompting.	Clarification of issues.
	Acknowledgment.	New ideas exchanged.
	Rapport.	New information received.
	Conversation management.	
	Facilitation.	
Responsibility elsewhere.	Acknowledgment.	Understanding of organization's commitment and remit.
	Explaining mediation.	Understanding of pros and cons of different options.
	Coaching.	Sense of what "I" can do.
	Facilitation.	
Skepticism.	Explaining mediation.	Understanding of mediation opportunity.
	Coaching.	Willingness to try.
	Patience.	
Fear.	Empathy.	Checking.
	Questioning.	Responding.
	Pacing.	Moving on.
	Creating a safe environment.	Gaining in confidence.
Tears.	Empathy.	Sense of relief.
	Reflection.	Feelings of achievement.
	Facilitation.	Needs being met.
		Ability to make agreements.

for only talking and listening really achieve anything different and lasting?

- **Win/lose psychology**—if I have to give something up then I know I have lost.
- **Transference of responsibility**—people are aware of their rights and the organization's responsibilities and we are reluctant to believe that we must resolve our own disputes. Resolving disputes is what procedures, line managers, and senior managers are there to do for us.
- **A perception that mediation is justice on the cheap**—we often believe that we are being fobbed off with something that is going to save the organization the money that it would have to pay us if we went down the formal routes. Management is running scared and is only trying to avoid compensation payouts, or costly changes in procedures and staffing.
- **A culture of blame**—which makes people afraid of any type of disclosure or acceptance of personal responsibility.

As people enter a mediation process they will need straightforward, understandable information about mediation so that they can make informed choices about whether or not to use it. However, whatever written information you produce, people will still have misgivings and may form unrealistic impressions of what is expected of them and of what mediators do. The task of encouraging disputants to try mediation falls on the manager, whether they are suggesting formal mediation or a mediation-type approach.

CASE STUDY
"HE'LL NEVER LISTEN"

Raj wanted to sort out some problems with his co-worker Kim, but was afraid of being verbally abused by her if he tried to talk things through on his own. He went to Peter, his manager, but expected little since when raising a similar issue with a previous boss, Ken, he had been fended off: "I am sure a grown man like you needn't worry on that score, Raj," and "Well, there has been a lot of bad feeling between you, Kim has strong feelings I know. You need to toughen up a bit."

Instead, Peter took the time to draw out Raj's concerns so that both of them were clear what was preventing Raj from wanting to go forward. Peter then went on to comment that a different approach was possible if Raj was willing to try it, namely mediation. He explained that it might be possible to have a meeting that was structured and had groundrules, so that Kim and Raj would both be clear from the outset what the parameters were. He gave the information in manageable chunks when Raj was ready to hear. He emphasized the groundrules, which made clear that verbal abuse was out of bounds, and he explained that the role he would be taking on would be to try to help both Raj and Kim say what they needed to, in a way that allowed the other to listen. It helped Raj to reflect that, by agreeing to this meeting, Kim would be agreeing up front to those groundrules. Finally, Peter emphasized that Raj would not be forced to continue if he was uncomfortable.

The manager's role is to explore people's expectations about mediation, first of all to check if these are accurate. It may be that giving a clear description of what happens in mediation, what mediators do, and what each person can get out of it is all that is required. People in a conflict are frequently more emotional than they may care to concede and have underlying anxieties about what might take place. Rather than offering reassurance, which managers can give in bucket loads without a drop being accepted by the disputant, managers need to acknowledge those concerns using empathy and rapport, before going on to target their message to that person's needs and explain how mediation can be of benefit to them.

CASE STUDY
"I SIMPLY DON'T HAVE THE TIME"

Carol, a busy senior manager facing a grievance from a junior member of her team, told Eve, an HR manager fully trained in mediation, that she was far too busy to mediate and was prepared to defend her corner if the grievance was brought forward. After listening and acknowledging Carol's position, Eve encouraged her to estimate the amount of time a formal complaint would take, versus a couple of hours in a mediation meeting. Together they ran through what a formal complaint might involve Carol in and the possible outcomes of that.

Eve emphasized the positive aspects of mediation, explaining what it can do. She made sure these were relevant to Carol—a personalized response is far more effective in encouraging someone to mediate than a standard one. For Carol, this meant hearing that mediation had a good chance of getting everyone back functioning as an effective team with some future groundrules.

Eve then appealed to Carol's status needs, as senior staff often find it hard to give up their authority during a mediation. She emphasized that Carol would make her own decisions, that she was in charge of what she said and how she responded, and that she could ask for a private meeting with Eve whenever she wished. She checked that Carol understood the confidentiality of the process and talked through examples of success. Finally Eve gave Carol time to think things over.

Two days later Carol agreed to give an hour to the meeting. In the event the mediation went on for three hours, which was largely at Carol's suggestion, as after the initial hour she was convinced of its usefulness to her and was happy to make that time available.

KEY LEARNING POINTS

■ Mediators learn to build understanding as they build rapport, through persistent, careful explanation, and also by being sensitive to parties' concerns about mediation.

■ Realize that parties have strong emotions about their disputes, may be in a fragile or volatile condition, and are unlikely to embrace mediation enthusiastically.

■ Ensure that you have given people all the information they need to enable them to make an informed choice and encourage them at least to "give it a go," as people who were in their situation have been surprised at how positive mediation was for them.

■ If parties choose to decline mediation, respect that choice and don't judge them on it.

REFERENCES

1   Hearn, J & Parkin, W (2001) *Gender, Sexuality and Violence in Organizations*, Sage, London.

Part II
Mediation in Action

In this part of the book we concentrate on the mediation process and mediation skills.

Chapter 4 maps out the mediation process using a case study. It works like a trailer to a film. Chapters 5–7 are the main feature, a one-to-one dispute between a new manager and a long-serving team member. Please be patient: It is detailed, demanding, and dramatic, but it does have a happy ending.

Chapters 8 and 9 then illustrate two applications of mediation: resolving a high-conflict situation involving allegations of sexism and bullying; and managing a group dispute.

4
A Map of the Process

Formal mediation has three blocks:

1 Talking separately and confidentially to the parties in dispute.
2 Considering whether the situation is suitable for mediation and whether the right people are involved.
3 Meeting with all the parties together.

People often make the mistake of considering that mediation only occurs in the last block, with the parties together. In fact, mediation begins at the first contact with the parties. At this stage many disputes are started firmly on the road to resolution. For many people in a dispute, the experience of talking to a mediator, hearing their story reflected back, and being encouraged to identify their interests helps them to take decisions about their situation. These might include talking to the other party directly, or recognizing an interest that can be met in a different way.

We have known parties who, after the separate sessions, have met in a corridor. One person has made a comment to the effect that "Surely we can work this out now," and they have talked things through there and then.

THE SEQUENCE OF MEDIATION

CHECKLIST
THE STAGES OF MEDIATION

Block 1: SEPARATE SESSIONS
Stage 1: First contact with the first party.
Stage 2: First contact with the second party.

Block 2: ASSESSMENT
Stage 3: Assessing the best way forward/preparation for setting up
   a joint meeting.

Block 3: JOINT MEETING
Stage 4: Setting the scene and hearing the issues.
Stage 5: Exploring and working on the issues.
Stage 6: Building agreements.
Stage 7: Closure.

STAGES 1 AND 2: FIRST CONTACT WITH THE PARTIES

During Stages 1 and 2 the intention, skills, and approach of the mediator are identical. The purpose of these two stages is to provide a safe, confidential place for parties to reflect individually and privately on:

- What has happened.
- How they are feeling.
- How to move forward.
- Can mediation and a win/win approach help?

STAGE 3: ASSESSMENT AND SETTING UP A JOINT MEETING

Stage 3 allows more time to:

- Set up the joint meeting at a mutually convenient time and place, if the parties have agreed to mediate and it is appropriate.
- Continue checking and assessing the situation and consulting with the parties or other stakeholders.
- Build commitment to the process if the parties and/or mediator are unsure about continuing.

■ Help the parties consider alternatives if the parties and/or mediator do not see a benefit in continuing.

■ Let the parties know the reason for not continuing, if that is the mediator's decision.

During joint mediation sessions on neutral territory the disputants are encouraged to continue in reflective mode for a little longer.

STAGE 4: SETTING THE SCENE AND HEARING THE ISSUES

In Stage 4, parties are asked to reflect, one at a time, in their different ways on:

■ What has happened.
■ How they are feeling.
■ Their key concerns and issues.
■ How to move forward.

STAGE 5: EXPLORING AND WORKING ON THE ISSUES

Stage 5 moves gently into a more interactive phase. Up to this point the communication has largely been through the mediator. Now the parties are invited to have a limited exchange of:

■ Ideas.
■ Feelings.
■ Information.
■ Understanding.

STAGE 6: BUILDING AGREEMENTS AND RELATIONSHIPS

Stage 6 is the first truly progressive phase, as the parties are helped to participate in a frank, open, and honest full exchange, without damaging one another. The earlier steps are building the parties up, coaxing and coaching them toward this. They are asked to exchange:

■ Ideas.
■ Feelings.
■ Information.
■ Understanding.
■ Ways of moving forward.

Stage 7 reaps the harvest of the exchange. It encourages the parties to move on to:

■ Planning mutually acceptable outcomes.
■ Building agreements that are comprehensive, workable, and fully understood.
■ Where that is not possible, moving on to considering what will happen next.
■ Closing as constructively as possible on the issues, the interaction, and the process.

THE MEDIATION DYNAMIC

The dynamic that is set up by this structure is very different from what often happens in negative conflict. As outlined in Chapter 2, life in the conflict zone often includes poor communication, clashes of values and beliefs, and hostile or defensive behaviors. Broadly speaking, interactive mediation asks the parties to **Reflect**, **Exchange** and **Move on**.

Reflection prepares people for exchange. By being held in an exploratory space people have the opportunity to say what they need to, identify what is important for them, and feel truly heard, understood, and valued. Too many attempts to resolve disputes are damaged by unprepared, defensive, or aggressive exchanges. The separate sessions with the parties, and the early stages of the joint session, invite people into a non-aggressive dialogue during which they are able to recap on events, reveal feelings, rehearse what they really want to say to the others, and reflect on what is truly important to them.

When involved in conflict, people often switch on negative filters. This means that they allow their prior views, beliefs, and values about the type of person in front of them to act as a lens through which they see that person. Normally we strive to challenge racist or stereotypical views, but sometimes they are almost automatic. When I was driving through the Tottenham area of London one afternoon a black man in a new BMW pulled out suddenly in front of me. How many of us would have had the same instant reaction as I did: "He looks like a drug dealer"? This is a negative filter from messages we have heard over and over, and is not at all a genuine response to the person and situation in front of us.

We all resent being hidden behind filters rather than being seen as who we are, and this makes us feel defensive, which, for many, means that we fight back. Or we switch off altogether and refuse to get involved because we see other people as intransigent or insensitive. The person with whom we are in conflict becomes someone we simply try to avoid emotionally, physically, and psychologically. Under these circumstances communication is difficult and often unproductive.

Mediation puts off the exchange until people feel ready for it, are starting to see through the negative filters, and feel safe enough to embark on the exchange with an element of hope, no matter how small. The rapport-building skills of the mediator in individual and joint sessions, and the conflict-management skills applied throughout, create a bridge between warring camps.

MOVE ON

Once the exchange begins, something and someone usually moves. Movement often occurs in people who are now focusing on the future rather than the past, or shifting from discussing positions to describing interests. Or they move from blame to recognition of differences. The dynamic created in mediation is usually so positive that even if no practical resolution is possible, communication improves and people are able to coexist in the workplace.

Mediators are not the arbiters of reality, but the agents of reality in mediation. They do not make decisions for people, but encourage them to focus on what is realistic and what they can change, and help the parties to come up with ideas that might work for everyone involved.

CASE STUDY
MEDIATION AT FIRST SIGHT

The mediation involved senior executives in an organization delivering an established, customer-focused insurance business through direct selling and a network of regional customer centers. The organization had pulled together a diverse, competent senior management team, generally seen by staff as enlightened and progressive.

The chief executive had described the current conflict as "like a whirlpool, sucking in even the strongest and most resistant, and dragging them down." Every attempt to resolve it had floundered, as people seemed upset and disoriented by the conflict, but too busy or too distant from one another geographically to "get together on this." Two senior managers were avoiding one another and communication generally was becoming frostier. Regional variations were also starting to creep into working practices, as certain senior managers were taking their teams their own way. The conflict was starting to have a negative impact on the business and the chief executive felt that the time was ripe to tackle it once and for all, using an "away day" for senior managers.

In this instance the person taking on the mediator role, Terry, was a new senior manager who had joined the organization recently and had previously been trained as a mediator. He was a peer, but was not really seen as part of the conflict. He sought permission from the chief executive to speak with each person privately on the phone to see whether they might be open to a joint mediation meeting.

KEY LEARNING POINT

If a conflict is well developed, the mediation process works best when you are a mediating manager who is not directly involved in the issues and can be seen as independent. Generally, using this approach early will reduce the risk of your being seen as a mediating manager who is in any way tainted by the conflict.

STAGES 1 AND 2: SEPARATE SESSIONS— FIRST CONTACT WITH EACH OF THE PARTIES

*Terry spoke to all managers involved on the phone, in random order. At this stage he **summarized and acknowledged** feelings, issues, and perceptions, and **collected initial ideas about ways forward**. He **built rapport** and **explained mediation**, emphasizing the benefits to each person according to their main anxieties. Terry **clarified feelings**, used **gentle questioning** to find out more information if necessary for him to understand, but **stayed impartial**, avoiding any requests for opinions, sympathy, or judgment.*

*These phone calls allowed each person to talk about the conflict, but **reflective listening** also encouraged people to evaluate their situation and think about ways forward. Terry was **patient**, listening to concerns and encouraging people to assess for themselves the benefits of seeking to resolve the conflict, against the risks of not giving it some dedicated attention. Little by little he **built commitment** to the mediation process. By listening first to their concerns and feelings he **established trust**, and one by one they agreed to go forward with the joint meeting.*

Issues

■ *A culture of fairly aggressive feedback had crept into the team, who would routinely pick holes in one another's ideas and rarely give positive feedback. Emails had figured quite heavily in this.*

■ *Strategic performance measures and targets were being set in a way that took little account of regional variations, e.g., the distribution of wealth in any one area, or resistance to traditional concepts of insurance. Certain managers felt that their good work was not being recognized by these figures and that other, more fruitful regions were being unfairly favored.*

■ *People were regularly missing conference calls designed to network information, whereas in the past these had been extremely productive and attendance at them had been 100 percent. The longest-serving manager, Sara, commented, "Desks were cleared, mountains moved so that people could stay in touch before. Now no one wants to meet, even down a phone line with hundreds of miles in between."*

People variously described their feelings as "boiling," "not bothered," "alienated," "insulted," and "misunderstood." They used fairly provocative language when referring to some of the history, and there were various ideas about who was to blame and what should be done to them. Many sound reasons were given about why focusing on the conflict would be "a waste of time," "doomed to failure," "only partly useful," or "OK for me, but Anil won't come." Several of the people involved thought that bringing in a mediator would be perceived as an admission of failure by their peers. There was a general fear that parading the conflict before a relative outsider would be humiliating and disempowering, and that nothing positive would come of it.

One of the purposes of separate, confidential conversations with each party is to assess with them the feasibility of mediating—the ripeness of the conflict for this approach. As the conversations with the six senior managers unfolded, Terry was struck by how each individual was potentially powerful and capable in their own right, as they spoke of difficult situations they had managed well in the past. It was also clear how stuck, frustrated, and in some cases powerless this dispute had made them as individuals and as a team.

The one thing everyone agreed on was that the situation could not continue as it was. The conflict was becoming unbearable and its cost could no longer be contemplated. A once-strong group was fragmenting. The issues were also all within their control, so given the right set of circumstances they should have the skills and authority to make changes happen. (See pages 206–8 for more information on whether a mediation should go ahead.)

People started the joint meeting anxiously and during each person's uninterrupted time there were some angry exchanges, which Terry managed to **control** without blaming. He acknowledged how people felt and **encouraged them to keep communicating** until they fully understood one another's positions. He concentrated on reflection and then summarized each person's key issues, concerns, and feelings, checking them back with the speaker.

Feelings

STAGE 3: ASSESSMENT

STAGE 4: SETTING THE SCENE AND HEARING THE ISSUES

STAGE 5: EXPLORING AND WORKING ON THE ISSUES

Once everyone had spoken, Terry asked some **clarifying questions** to **identify issues and positions** before moving on. He **encouraged initial, general dialogue** between the managers and together they succeeded in moving from a series of statements to a list of issues that they all agreed needed to be addressed (see page 103, Framing the issues). Terry and the group set out a positively framed **agenda** outlining their aims for the next stage.

STAGE 6: BUILDING AGREEMENTS AND RELATIONSHIPS

Taking **one issue at a time**, Terry **facilitated** an open, honest exchange, shifting people into a less blaming, more tolerant gear. Everyone present understood much more fully why people had found it difficult to talk. For example, some felt particularly under pressure because of the performance-measurement system; others felt bolstered by it. This had not been something they had been able to talk about in the past without blaming each other, or labeling each other as "wrong," "arrogant," or "stupid." Even though people did get angry, Terry was able to **control the interactions**, keep people to the **groundrules**, and **support** everyone in saying what they needed to in a non-blaming way, which allowed the others to hear their point rather than simply responding to their anger.

Terry helped everyone identify a **common goal**, which for this issue was how they could all ensure that strategic monitoring could happen appropriately and constructively, to produce knowledge and learning, not opportunities for inappropriate competition. He then moved the group into option-generating mode, and a couple of ideas were highlighted for further evaluation. Leaving this issue to one side, Terry then went back over the agenda and repeated the process for each area of concern.

STAGE 7: CLOSURE

After all the issues had been discussed and a handful of options put on the table, the managers were ready to **evaluate and select** specific ways forward. This they were able to do with Terry **encouraging** them through difficulties, reminding them of the progress made to date, and **reiterating the purpose of mediation** when things appeared to be stuck. **Agreements** were made on all the issues, which the group asked Terry to *write down for each manager as an aide memoire of the meeting. Terry also encouraged them to think about **fall-back** positions, and about what would happen if these arrangements did not work out in practice.*

The managers were keen to discuss their experience of mediation and were asked to feed back to Terry what had helped. Their comments were an interesting mixture:

FEEDBACK

- *"His resolve and attention to detail kept me going."*
- *"Such a relief; people started listening again."*
- *"The structure made sense. We really did need to see the problem from all angles first, before trying to devise ways forward."*
- *"The solution was contained in the conflict. We had been looking for people from outside to help, but we were the experts—and the mediator helped us realize that."*

KEY LEARNING POINTS

- Left alone in the conflict zone, people fight, get stuck, ignore, and often give up on one another. To offer something different, the mediator must be seen to be outside the conflict. You cannot mediate conflicts in which you are directly involved—although mediation skills will still be valuable; see Chapter 10.
- Allow enough time before seeking forward movement. People are more ready to exchange ideas and feelings constructively when they first have had a chance to reflect on the issues, feelings, and options.
- Exchanges can become heated, but that does not mean that they are going nowhere. The toughest but most important job for mediators is to work out when not to interrupt an argument; see Chapter 7, Moving on.
- When forward movement does emerge develop it, affirm it, and focus on the future.

5

Working with the Parties Separately

One main case study will take you through the first two stages of the mediation process, highlighting:

- Key concepts and skills.
- Important stages in the process.
- Learning points.

CASE STUDY
ENVIRONMENTAL PROJECTS

Setting

Environmental Projects (EP) is a government body seeking to work with businesses, individuals, environmentalists, and politicians toward an agenda of appropriate development and planning. It has 6,000 staff in the UK and a European division that offers consultancy across northern Europe. There are 150 project officers across the UK, many of whom have been working with EP for eight to ten years. Recently procedures have been adopted to ensure monitoring and evaluation of project work and appraisal of individual performance, and several new managers have been recruited to lead project teams but also to establish a new professionalism within the ranks. The project officers are recognized as technically gifted and leaders in their respective fields. Several of them are suspicious of the new managers, and some of them had applied, unsuccessfully, for the new posts.

Bryan was recruited into EP as a new manager a year ago. He had worked in the retail industry and town planning, and had recently taken an MBA, specializing in performance management.

Victor has been a project officer for 11 years. He worked in the former East Germany as a technical adviser to the petrochemical industry and built up a portfolio of impressive publications on river pollution. He is used to working for a regional manager, Betty, who largely left it to him to organize his own work schedule.

Four team members have independently reported to Betty friction between Bryan and Victor. Betty had not previously thought that this was a significant problem, although she had expected initial tension between them, since Victor had hoped to get the team leader's job himself. Betty also knows that the team members mentioned above were not inclined to raise issues about colleagues unless they are deeply affected. A couple of key incidents have been mentioned, one involving a bitter exchange in a team meeting. The other was seen by only two team members, as Victor and Bryan had a heated discussion in the team's open-plan office about Victor not turning up to a key site meeting. The team members all believed that the friction was seriously affecting the working spirit and sense of unity in the team.

The day after the fourth report from staff, Bryan emailed Betty to seek her advice about disciplining Victor. Betty thought that this was a perfect case for mediation.

This frosty situation had gone on unchecked for a year. Other team members had waited until they could tolerate no more, but they still needed outside help, feeling that it was not their place to intervene. No one else had been notified or involved until the staff went to Betty. Bryan was considering moving to disciplinary procedures, but had not started the process yet.

Betty takes on the mediator role, as she now line manages Bryan and was also Victor's line manager for years. She was on the recruitment panel for Bryan, but is not seen as part of the history or content of this dispute. She has been around for longer than both and has not had to cross swords previously with either. Betty is aware, however, that her rank makes her closer to Bryan but that, conversely, Bryan may feel that Victor is "her man." She will have to be careful to establish her impartiality.

It is important for Betty to set up the process confidently, explaining how she will be working and what is expected of the

Previous attempts at resolution

Setting up individual meetings

parties. Betty begins by phoning them both to schedule meetings that will:

- *Allow her to get a picture of what has been happening from each person's perspective.*
- *Help identify any issues that may be affecting how Bryan and Victor are working together.*
- *Explore the possibility of working on these issues together through mediation.*

Betty uses similar phrases with both Bryan and Victor, to ensure fairness and consistency. Bryan quickly agrees to see her. Betty knows that she will have to be really clear with Bryan about her role, and in particular how she is seeking to resolve the situation without the need for disciplinary action. Of course, Victor is curious about why she wants to meet them and what she has heard, but agrees to see Betty. She notes that Victor will need an opportunity to express his skepticism, and that she will need to ensure that she is appropriately encouraging without being over-pushy.

KEY LEARNING POINTS
GETTING PEOPLE TO AGREE TO MEET A MEDIATING MANAGER

- It is never a good idea either to get someone to mediation on false pretenses, or to coerce people into taking part.
- Keeping attendance at mediation on a voluntary basis is crucial to the parties' commitment to and ownership of the issues and the outcomes.
- Avoid getting into detailed discussion of the issues when setting up individual sessions with the parties.
- Build rapport without losing impartiality.
- Give consistent and clear information about the process.

Table 5 Stages 1 and 2: First contact with the parties

Aims	Core skills
Encouraging people to reflect individually and privately on:	1 Setting the scene and building rapport.
■ What has happened.	2 Reflective listening.
■ How they are feeling.	3 Getting people outside their conflict zone.
■ How to move forward.	4 Encouraging people to mediate.
■ Whether or not a mediation-style approach can help.	5 Impartiality.

CORE SKILL 1: SETTING THE SCENE AND BUILDING RAPPORT

When we ask people what helps them trust mediators in the early stages of the process, they say that it helps when mediators are:

■ Welcoming and confident.
■ Clear about their role.
■ Able to listen to concerns about the process and deal with any questions or challenges constructively.

THE CONCEPT

As the process progresses, it is the mediator's listening skills and ability to demonstrate empathy that build rapport. Once you have established this connection you can influence the parties, for example by inviting them to look at a situation differently, asking them to move from blame to outcome, or encouraging them to see the benefits of mediation.

Rapport exists on many levels and the type you establish in mediation is different, for example, from that existing between good friends, siblings, or intimate partners. If you have spent time in a taxi, you will have experienced the various ways taxi drivers communicate with their passengers. Some people may want a conversation, but they are unlikely to have taken a taxi to get a lecture or a monologue. Those drivers who launch into their often colorful opinions about life, society, and the world, and do not get a full-on response are not pitching their communication appropriately. At home, or down the pub with mates, strong views exchanged vigorously may suit the group norms, but with a captive, paying passenger, the taxi driver is not operating at an appropriate level of rapport.

Rapport is about pitching communication at the right level, noticing the reaction, and tailoring communication to the person and the situation.

THE SKILL

When people are involved in conflicts it is easy for them to feel belittled and deskilled. People will often seek reassurance, confirmation, and in some cases advice from mediators. They are even more likely to want it from mediating managers. However, the minute you give people what they want your impartiality is gone. As a rule of thumb, not responding at all will not work. People will feel ignored and rapport will decrease. The trick is to respond without losing impartiality.

Mediators build rapport without breaching impartiality by:

- Demonstrating interest and attention.
- Active listening.
- Establishing and maintaining empathy.
- Use of space, silence, and pacing.
- Signposting the process.
- Tailoring communication and the process to different people's needs.
- Remaining calm under pressure.
- Establishing a safe environment.
- Building confidence in their ability to sustain the process of dialogue under pressure.
- Staying positive in the face of adversity.

At Betty's private meeting with Bryan he is keen to get started, so she keeps her introduction brief but does emphasize her role at this stage as mediator not investigator. She stresses confidentiality, and that she needs to hear Victor's version of events, and then hopefully get Victor and Bryan together. Victor is more reluctant at the beginning and Betty spends more time with him exploring his concerns and acknowledging his feelings about her role.

She also says more about impartiality, as this is more relevant to him. Bryan invites her to agree with his opinion: "Betty, you know Victor well. He has a tendency toward arrogance, doesn't he?"

Betty initially hands that back to Bryan: "Perhaps you believe that, Bryan. What makes you think that?"

When Bryan persists, she has to clarify her role: "I can see, Bryan, that you want me to comment on Victor, but it wouldn't help. Imagine if Victor asked me to agree with his opinion of you. What we are dealing with here are the practicalities of working together and I can see that you have strong feelings about Victor's attitude to you. Can we get back to that?"

KEY LEARNING POINTS
BUILDING RAPPORT IN THE EARLY STAGES

- ■ Use a checklist to help you introduce your role consistently, clearly, and briefly, but be prepared to be flexible.
- ■ Work with people's concerns early on.
- ■ Use the following behaviors to build rapport early in meetings:
  - — Be welcoming and positive.
  - — Check people's comfort and needs.
  - — Adopt open, positive body language.
  - — Explain about note taking, if you intend to take notes.
  - — Use a couple of rapport-building questions if appropriate, e.g., "Did you find your way here OK?"

CORE SKILL 2: REFLECTIVE LISTENING

THE CONCEPT

We are all extremely good at creating our own versions of reality. We "fill in the gaps" in communication, as well as assuming that people attach the same meanings to words as we do and share our map of the world. It is the perceptions of reality and the misunderstandings and assumptions that we create that often lie at the center of conflict.

There are two key ways in which we make sense of what other people say and do, selective perception and adaptive perception.[1]

We pay attention to only a part of what we are seeing and

Selective perception

exclude other information. We choose what to notice, lose other information, and fill in the gaps. Selective perception acts as a kind of shorthand, which helps us to manage, and understand, the wealth of data that comes at us.

The biggest shortcoming of selective perception is that it often causes us to make false assumptions, or miss key pieces of information because they do not seem important to us. Selective perception may go undetected, but *selective listening* will not. We focus on what is important for us, lose much of what the speaker says, and misuse much more. It is disastrous to rapport, and prevents effective information gathering and inhibits understanding of feelings.

Adaptive perception

Adaptive perception involves filtering new things, people, and situations that we encounter through our existing base of knowledge and experience. This allows us to compare, contrast, and judge other people's experience alongside our own. We also put others' experience into context, for example by ranking (placing it as more or less valuable or noteworthy) and risk assessing (working out how much of a threat it may or may not be).

Adaptive perception can be a valuable defense mechanism and safety device in humans, allowing us to size up situations and people quickly. Sadly, it also leads to judgmental attitudes, closed thinking, and resistance to behavior and thinking that are outside our norms. When this style of perception strongly influences our listening, it creates a gap between the speaker and listener and a misapprehension of what is important for the speaker. The listener will often start probing areas of interest to him or her, rejecting the validity of the speaker's experience and using leading questions and judgmental language.

A good example of adaptive perception is the commonplace situation of a man—let's call him Jim—going to a conference where he is hoping to meet Dr. O'Brien. The receptionist points out a woman sitting at a table. Jim goes over and says, "Hello love, will Dr. O'Brien be joining you in a moment? He didn't say he was bringing his PA."

Getting the whole story

Mediators create a reflective space in which people can feel truly valued and express clearly what is happening, how it is affecting them, and what is important to them. It also allows mediators to detach themselves from the material without losing interest or sacrificing empathy. In reflective listening the mediating manager's concern is:

- To get the full story.
- To show that you understand what is causing the conflict.
- To appreciate the effect that this is having on the parties.
- To get a full picture of what the parties need and how they think the conflict can be managed and the dispute resolved.

CHECKLIST
THE BENEFITS OF REFLECTIVE LISTENING

- The parties feel they have space to say what is important to them.
- They are not being judged.
- They can plainly see that someone is seeking to listen well and understand.
- They have the opportunity to reflect on what has happened and what they are thinking and feeling about themselves and others.
- They can feel better having got everything out into the open.
- They can move on from identifying issues to selecting ways forward.

Reflective listening involves:

THE SKILL

- Paying attention and being open to a wide range of experiences.
- Listening as though you are a clean sheet, waiting to be filled.
- Using accurate and appropriate summaries of information and feelings.
- Using appropriate questioning (the funnel technique, see below).

People in a dispute will be talking about the same events, but may well concentrate on different aspects. When mediating disputes we cannot allow ourselves to close out or not be open to certain versions of events because we have already made up our mind. The credibility of the speaker is not the issue; it is what they are thinking, feeling, and saying about events. In

Paying attention and being open to a wide range of experiences many social and professional activities we do assess people's credibility and will often doubt the validity of some people's experience because the content, manner of expression, or sequencing of one person's story clashes with what we might consider normal or acceptable. In mediation we must remain open to varying accounts, concentrate on what is being described, and respect it by reflecting it, not distorting it.

Listening as though you are a clean sheet

Mediators treat every situation initially as though they know nothing. This allows them to pay attention, avoid adaptive and selective listening, and encourage maximum disclosure from the speaker. Encouragement both verbally ("Thanks for that," "Help me understand," "I'd really like to know") and non-verbally (open, attentive body language, steady nods, held but not constant eye contact) allows the listener to pay attention and gives the impression that they are "all ears." It will not work if you have all the body language but still do not pay attention, or let your own responses flood into your mind.

Genuine clean sheet listening helps draw people out, avoids prejudging, and contributes significantly to rapport. It never ceases to amaze us what people are prepared to disclose if they are really listened to in this way.

Using accurate and appropriate summaries

Summaries are used regularly in mediation in order to:

■ Check and clarify.
■ Show that the mediator is clearly listening.
■ Seek feedback on what you have been hearing so far.
■ Help people move on.

Summaries are employed when:

■ A great deal of information is coming across and you need to pause and clarify.
■ The pacing needs to be slowed down.
■ Feelings are present that need to be acknowledged.
■ Mediators are seeking to move people forward in the process or content (see page 80–3 on getting the second party on board).

CHECKLIST
EFFECTIVE SUMMARIES

Effective summaries…

■ Are tentative, presented as the listener's version, to be checked with the speaker.
■ Include a combination of fact and feelings.
■ Acknowledge and affirm feelings.
■ Include all the main issues.
■ Include important phrases that other parties have used.
■ Avoid being patronizing or changing the content.
■ Avoid loaded phrases.
■ Reduce the content without minimizing the significance.
■ Use neutral language that conveys meaning without blaming or labeling.
■ Are checked with the parties for confirmation or otherwise.

Questions are one of the mediator's most valuable tools. They allow us to explore other people's experience, stay open to it, and demonstrate interest and attention. The purpose of questioning in mediation is to build rapport and understanding of the situation as the party sees it. Questions can also be used to give the party an opportunity to choose to view things differently.

Questions can be open or closed. It is the purpose of the question and not the grammar that decides whether a question is open or not. "Could you tell me everything that happened?" is an open question as it seeks a broad, narrative response. "What is the time?" can be answered without using "yes" or "no," but this does not make it an open question, since it is only seeking a narrow response.

Open questions enable others to elaborate on their own experience. There are two main types, door openers and open prompts.

Once given a starting signal, some people do not need much encouragement to share their life experiences with you. As a mediator you will often be in the privileged position of honored listener, there at the right time to hear a story that

Using appropriate questioning

Open questions

desperately needs to be told and heard. Once you have set the scene the speaker will pour out their account. If this is not the case and one of the parties is reluctant, open questions and open prompts can be very useful to get the speaker started.

Table 6 Open questions: door openers and open prompts

Door opener
"So talk us through what's been happening."
"What has life been like at work?"
"In your own words, describe everything you can remember about…"

Open prompt
"Tell me more."
"What happened next?"
"And then?"

Door opener for feelings
"How did that affect you?"
"What are your feelings about that?"

Open prompt for feelings
"Say a little more about your feelings if you can."
"Could you give me an example of when you felt like that?"

Closed questions help people focus and constructively limit what they say. There are three main types:

■ Specifying questions help people get their experience across with more clarity, accuracy, and precision.
■ Challenging questions seek to clarify connections and the relevance of the content to the desired outcome.
■ Closing questions seek to achieve closure on an issue, an option, or a perception.

The funnel technique

As the opening narrative slows, repetition sets in, or time constraints require more focus, you need to summarize essential information, feelings, issues, and emerging points. Now is the time to use more focused questions, moving "down the funnel" from narrative to the real issues (see Figure 4).

Table 7 Closed questions

General clarification	"When you say…, what do you mean?"
	"Could you give me an example of…?"
Timescale	"So bring me up to date. What's the situation like now?"
	"Was there ever a time when things were better?"
	"How was it early on?"
Feelings	"You said that this has affected your work. In what way?"
	"How have your feelings changed?"
Checking perceptions	"So in your eyes X was a bad manager? Did he ever talk to you about how he was going to manage you?"
	"Did the team know what to expect from the manager? What would you expect from a good manager?"
Challenging questions	"Can you think of anything you might be doing to contribute to this situation?"
	"Have you made your concerns known directly to X? What was his reaction?"
Closing questions	"So you are convinced that X was doing this deliberately?"
	"So… is the main issue for you?"
	"Is there anything else you would like to tell me?"
	"Are you ready to move on to looking at ways forward now?"

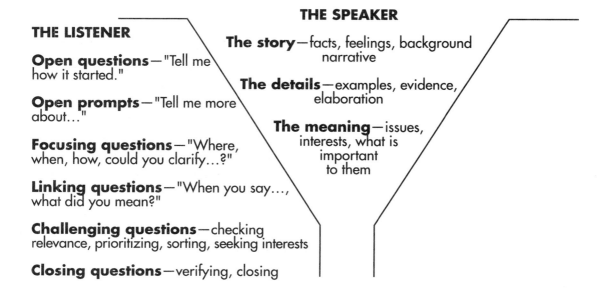

Figure 4 The funnel technique

CHECKLIST
QUESTIONING GUIDELINES

■ Start with open questions and leave space for people to express themselves. Use open prompt questions to continue the story in the speaker's own words.

■ Once you have reflected the essential ingredients of the narrative account, use closed questions to establish meaning. Avoid too many questions too soon, and too many questions in a row.

■ Use the "funnel technique," gradually moving from open to more closed questions in order to encourage speakers to move from a narrative to a more issue-focused description of what their concerns are.

■ Use probing, not prying, questions. Think why you need to ask this question. Probing gets you the information you need, while accepting that there are some areas where it may not be advisable to go.

■ Ensure that questions do not carry judgment or blame.

■ Be sensitive and responsive to people's needs. If questions are not producing disclosure and rapport is going down, ease off the pacing and level of focus.

Closed questions help establish the parties' exact issues, feelings, and concerns. By this stage people often feel that they have been accurate and detailed in their disclosure, and that the mediator has taken in as much as possible.

The mediator will now give a second summary, this time concentrating on key issues rather than detailed feedback. Key new information will probably be highlighted here, as well as any corrections from the earlier summary. The time is now ripe for reflecting on ways forward and explaining the mediation process.

Once he understood the purpose of the meeting and Betty's role in it, Bryan needed little prompting. In fact, he was full of indignation and quite dejected.

When he ran out of steam, Betty summarized: "Bryan, you felt that Victor was disappointed from the start that he did not get the manager's job, and, more pointedly for you, he felt that someone with technical expertise should have got it. A couple of times he hinted at this in team meetings, but recently he has been more direct, questioning your judgment, and also your right to dictate his work schedule.

"You mentioned that a recent incident a month ago had brought this to a head, when Victor did not turn up for a site meeting that you considered crucial, but were unable to attend yourself. Victor, by not attending, has, in your eyes, seriously jeopardized the chances of influencing the developer at that site. When you raised this with him quietly in the office, deliberately choosing a time when few people were around, he became hostile and refused to acknowledge that he had ever agreed to attend, saying that he 'had better things to do.'

"Generally speaking, you said that the approach Victor has taken to you has not been worrying or affecting the team. Recently, though, you described Victor's attitude to you as 'undermining' and growing 'ever more publicly disdainful.' Clearly this is affecting you a great deal. You sounded frustrated, Bryan, and you want some changes in behavior from Victor. You are on the verge of taking disciplinary action. Is that an accurate summary?"

Bryan confirmed that it was.

KEY LEARNING POINTS

- Plan questions before mediating. The best questions are ones you can use in, or adapt to, a wide range of situations, and with a wide range of people.
- Test your questions out on others—check how they would feel if asked such a question. What are you hoping to achieve by it? Is there a more elegantly phrased question that could achieve the same purpose?
- In the separate sessions, and the first stage of the joint session, you are in reflective mode. Getting the situation clear from all perspectives is your primary goal, not working the material, assessing the credibility of the parties, or judging what they bring.

CORE SKILL 3: GETTING PEOPLE OUTSIDE THEIR CONFLICT ZONE

THE CONCEPT

In our experience far too many workplace conflicts get stuck because of adversarial thinking. In the conflict zone people adopt behaviors that make sense to them, but often lock them into a unproductive dialogue and sustain negative conflict. Formal investigations start from an assumption of mistrust, putting everyone and everything under the microscope. However, managers who mediate will be starting from a position of greater trust.

The assumption in mediation is that, given the right set of circumstances and a safe, non-adversarial arena, people will step out of their conflict zone into a state of mind, heart, and spirit where self-respect is possible and win/lose thinking and behavior are not necessary.

Positions and interests

"Your position is something you have decided upon. Your interests are what caused you to decide ... Reconciling interests rather than positions works for two reasons. First, for every interest there usually exists several possible positions that could satisfy it. All too often people simply adopt the most obvious position ... When you do look behind opposed for the motivating interests, you can often find an alternative position which meets not only your interests but theirs as well. [Second] We tend to assume that because the other side's positions are opposed to ours, their interests must also be opposed. In many negotiations, however, a close examination of the underlying interests will reveal the existence of many more interests that are shared or compatible rather than ones that are opposed."[2]

As soon as the issues are clear and the details of what is important are understood, the mediator can get to work unlocking positional thinking and uncovering interests.

THE SKILL

The skill of getting people outside their conflict zone involves:

- ■ Clarifying and acknowledging positions.
- ■ Extracting needs statements from blaming comments.
- ■ Exploring the interests behind positions.

Once people have finished giving their account of the situation they are asked to suggest some ways forward. At this stage positions often appear. An acknowledgment and a couple of checking questions give the speaker a chance to reflect on the position, and to clarify for themselves if that is what they actually want and how feasible it is.

Clarify and acknowledge positions

Table 8 Examples of position statements and checking questions

---

Position: "Sack him"

Possible mediator responses:

"You feel that strongly?"

"So your way forward is for X to be sacked? How realistic is that?"

"How might that change things for you?"

"What is good about that option for you?"

"Does that option have any drawbacks for you?"

Position: "Tell her to get a life"

Possible mediator responses:

"She's upset you a great deal. What do you mean, tell her to get a life?"

"Is that the best way to change the situation?"

"What, more specifically, does that mean for you? What behaviors are you asking that she takes on?"

Bryan and Victor are upset with one another and their comments to Betty are loaded with innuendo and blame. Betty doesn't react, but instead seeks to draw needs statements from the negative comments.

Bryan: "Victor thinks he's a gift from God."

Betty: "What makes you say that?"

Bryan: "He's arrogant and dismissive. Especially when he's contradicted."

Betty: "What do you want Victor to do, when you challenge or contradict him?" or "So what do you need from Victor?" or "What sort of changes are you after?"

Victor: "Bryan knows nothing. I knew more than he does when I was at school. He might be my boss, but he is out of his depth here."

Betty: "So you're in a difficult position. Your boss does not have the same technical expertise as you. What would make that

Extract needs statements from blaming comments

situation more manageable for you?" or "Does a manager necessarily need to know more than his team? What do you want from your manager?"

Bryan: "Victor wouldn't know teamwork if it hit him in the face." Betty: "What do you mean by teamwork? Have you ever talked to Victor about this? How did he react? What can you do to get more team working from him?"

Explore the interests behind positions

Interests are much more fruitful than positions, although less dramatic. It is useful to have a range of questions at your disposal to draw interests out. For example:

- ■ "Ideally, what would you like to come out of our discussions?"
- ■ "You mentioned that you think he is... How would you like him to be different? What do you need from him?"
- ■ "So you want him off your back? Why do you want that? What will it achieve? Can the team work without him?"
- ■ "Why is that important to you?"
- ■ "You mentioned 'professionalism.' What do you mean by that?"

As interests emerge, they need to be confirmed and reflected back.

Betty realizes that Bryan wants to get the most out of Victor, but needs more respect, particularly in public. He is not entirely clear how this will happen. He also wants to be seen to be consistent in the team. Bryan wants to work out a diary system with Victor, just as he has with every other member of the team. This is something Victor has resisted strongly before.

Victor needs some breathing space and reassurance that Bryan is not policing his every move. Betty is already beginning to notice that familiar human needs are at work here: the needs for respect, space, and good communication.

There is so much more negotiating room in interests than in the positions they hide behind. The mediator can see that already. Now she has to convince the parties that it would be beneficial for them to:

■ *Express their concerns directly to one another clearly and in a way that the other person can hear and understand.*
■ *Identify and sort out the issues between them.*
■ *Move beyond positions to interests.*
■ *Identify common interests.*
■ *Recognize and respect differences.*
■ *Respond to one another's concerns.*
■ *Work out ways in which they can both get their interests met.*

CORE SKILL 4: ENCOURAGING PEOPLE TO MEDIATE

THE CONCEPT

Not everyone is highly motivated when it comes to dispute resolution. Disputes often form an anchor for people's emotions and their perceptions of themselves and others. Take the conflict away and life loses a defining shadow. Resolve the dispute and it will be like losing an old friend.

As a mediating manager you should expect resistance to mediation, fueled by psychological and emotional factors. Practical concerns about mediation will also be evident, such as skepticism about results, misunderstanding of the purpose and format of mediation, and what to do if it does not work. You will need to become an effective communicator about, and advocate for, mediation.

THE SKILL

The separate sessions with the individual parties are primarily there so that they can reflect on their issues, feelings, and ways forward. As mentioned above, brief explanations of the mediator's role are given at the beginning of each separate session. Once the mediator has listened to and really understood the parties' stories, and worked on unlocking positional thinking, people are often more ready to listen to what the mediator has to say.

Betty has set up a dialogue combining open, honest communication, and a more reflective, less positional mindset, in each separate session. Bryan and Victor are both upset and need things to change, but, like many potential users of mediation, they have misgivings about using an unfamiliar way forward. Mediation still receives minimal public coverage, and because of its very nature it is unlikely that most people have ever been directly involved in it before. Betty now seeks to make Victor and Bryan more familiar with mediation.

Bryan thinks he will look bad if he accepts mediation. Betty checked on how, and discovered that Bryan knows that Victor went for his job and did not get it. Bryan did try to speak to Victor about this, but got the "cold shoulder." "One thing that can't be changed," said Bryan, "is the fact that I am his manager. I don't want any outsider coming in and telling me how to manage."

Betty explained that she would not be taking over. "In fact, although early on I may say quite a bit, you two will be doing most of the talking, as you know your situation best. This is about how you, Bryan, a manager, can work with Victor, one of your team, who also happened to go for your job. I want you both to tell each other how to move this situation forward."

Bryan is reassured about the mediator's role even more when Betty mentions that the sessions are confidential and that she will not be writing up the procedure. Bryan and Victor will control what, if anything, is disclosed. Bryan is still not convinced that Victor will "play ball." Betty asks Bryan to concentrate on his own commitment to the process, and highlights the potential benefits of mediation to him. We will shortly see how Betty works with Victor to build his commitment to mediation.

KEY LEARNING POINT
EXPLORE CONCERNS BEFORE EXPLAINING MEDIATION

When people have fears and concerns about mediation, don't just steamroller them with information. Remember the 3 Es:

■ Explore people's concerns—what are the factors causing them to feel anxiety or reluctance about mediation?

- Explain the relevant piece of information about mediation, to allay those concerns.
- Encourage them to see the benefits of mediation, with regard to their situation.

Bryan feels that the mediation process is offering him an opportunity that has some risks, but also that the benefits will outweigh the risks. He agrees to meet in a joint mediation session the next day, if Victor also agrees.

The benefits of mediation for Bryan are:

Benefits of mediation for Bryan

- *It will help him get his point across and gain a response, in a private, non-aggressive environment.*
- *It will be relatively speedy.*
- *This is not a technical dispute but one about communication and Bryan believes that mediation is more suited to this type of dispute than a more formal approach.*
- *The mediator has skills that neither Bryan nor Victor have been able to muster so far in this dispute, and Bryan believes that this will help move the situation along.*

CHECKLIST
COMMUNICATING ABOUT MEDIATION

- Describe what happens in mediation, what mediators do, and what the parties can get out of it.
- Emphasize the benefits of mediation and be realistic about its limitations.
- Use clear, easy to understand language.
- Give the information in manageable chunks when the party is ready to hear you.
- Target your message to that person's needs—explain how mediation can be of benefit to them.
- Be positive and say what mediation can do, e.g., "You will get an opportunity to make your own decisions" rather than "We will not make any decisions for you."

- Talk through examples of success.
- Help people assess the value of other methods of dispute resolution (e.g., litigation) alongside mediation.
- Stress that they are not forced to continue, if they are getting no satisfaction.
- Give them time to think things over if they appear reluctant to commit themselves.

The confidence and trust built by the mediator's communication and rapport-building skills form a significant factor in people's decision to go ahead with a joint mediation meeting. A couple of recent feedback forms from our dispute-resolution service highlight this:

- "She just gave me the confidence to be there, although I knew it would not be easy."
- "Without the mediator I couldn't have done it. With him I was more receptive, and felt much more optimistic that my boss would take my concerns on board."

KEY LEARNING POINTS
BENEFITS OF SEEING PARTIES SEPARATELY FIRST

This case highlights the importance of working with the parties individually before bringing them together. These separate reflective sessions allow the parties to:

- Be open, without feeling guilty or stupid.
- Explore and step back from the issues and feelings involved.
- Identify the pattern of conflict and style of communication that have so far prevailed.
- Understand the mediation-style approach and its benefits.
- Rehearse the style of communication requested during mediation.

CORE SKILL 5: IMPARTIALITY

Mediators need to manage—and step back from—their own responses to the people they work with and the material they come into contact with in their third-party role. As mentioned earlier, we all have the capacity to prejudge people and situations, to make assumptions and listen selectively and adaptively, under the influence of our own experience and values. This internal process of self-management comes under the concept of neutrality.

THE CONCEPT

We have identified 10 principles that help people maintain neutrality:

THE SKILL

1 Get to know your own buttons—the things that heat you up or freeze your skills.
2 Pay attention to your body—it will tell you when your feelings are affecting your thoughts and behavior.
3 Be aware of any patterns of behavior that might lead you into familiarly difficult territory, e.g., a tendency to rescue or protect.
4 Pay attention to the person in front of you.
5 Develop neutral language (see pages 134–6 for more on this).
6 Check out assumptions early on.
7 Come to each situation as a stranger who needs to know everything.
8 Ensure that you understand fully where someone is coming from (particularly if your views seem very close to theirs, or are strikingly different).
9 Monitor the amount and type of attention that you give people.
10 Take a break if you feel yourself getting drawn in or pushed out.

Impartiality is the visible sign of neutrality. Mediators are not robotic or cold. The skills mentioned so far should be utilized with all parties, irrespective of our sense of them. The steps of the process will also be repeated with all parties. It is this consistency of approach, and the removal of the notion of victim and perpetrator, protagonist and respondent, that gives mediation its transparently impartial quality.

CHECKLIST
ACTIVE IMPARTIALITY IN PRACTICE

■ Demonstrate interest and attention.
■ Allow people time to give you their own version of events, even when you already have an idea of what is going on.
■ Acknowledge feelings and seek to understand where all parties are coming from.
■ Resist getting drawn into arguments, offers, or pleas for sympathy.
■ Be balanced and fair in the way that the structure of the mediation process is applied.
■ Pay equal attention to different versions of events and different people.
■ Encourage maximum participation.
■ Plan questions and use questioning routines (see pages 68–71).
■ Be open to feedback on your impartiality and take it into account.

Bias

Victor comes second in the process and feels hard done by. "You're not likely to listen to me are you?" he moans. He also thinks that Betty will be on the manager's side, since she recruited him.

Betty is not upset, nor does she get defensive. She listens to Victor's concerns, acknowledges them, and asks what she can do to reassure him. He says that he feels forced to come and doubts that the mediation will get anywhere. Betty responds to each concern in turn.

Forced to attend

"I can understand you thinking that I am close to Bryan, but in my role as mediator I am not taking sides, or allowing any views I may or may not have, to intrude into a conflict that belongs to you and Bryan. I am just as interested in your version of events as Bryan's (pause) so tell me, what's been happening with you and Bryan, from your perspective?

"I am sorry that it felt as though you had no choice, Victor. This genuinely is an invitation. If you still felt at the end of today's session that you did not want to go ahead you would

have the right to stop the process and I would make sure that the choice remained confidential. I hope that you will see that this is actually a good opportunity to get your views across to Bryan, and be clear about what the issues are that he has with you. Then maybe you can get through this situation quickly and successfully for both of you.

"Talk to me about your issues, Victor, and what you think needs changing. This will be your opportunity to get your views across to Bryan, and for him to listen and respond. The idea of mediation is that both of you get a chance to settle any differences, not to attack each other or prove each other wrong."

Once Victor has described what has been going on for him, Betty emphasizes that mediation is a good opportunity to move things on. She will be there to maximize communication and explore every possibility. Victor is clearly upset, but uncertain about Bryan's motives. Betty now tells him that Bryan has agreed to a joint meeting. She and Victor discuss whether the cost of the conflict continuing is greater for both of them than any immediate discomfort they might feel about meeting one another.

Mediating managers like Betty demonstrate another important aspect of impartiality—balance—by letting all the parties know that the process is seeking to be fair, that mediation gives each of them the same opportunities, and asks them all to abide by the same rules. "This session is confidential, just as my session with Bryan was. You can tell me anything you like about the situation in your own words. Then we'll try to clarify what your issues are, and what you'd like to change."

Betty actively maintains her impartiality throughout. Her interest in Victor's version of events mirrors that demonstrated with Bryan. The slate is wiped clean and Victor gets a "good listening to," just as Bryan did. When Victor's version contradicts Bryan's, Betty reflects, asks follow-up questions and clarifies. It is not her job to start working on contradictions, challenging Victor's version, or pursuing Bryan's agenda. When those emerge in joint session Betty will help the parties work through them.

The first party, Bryan, was given reflective listening, so impartiality demands that Victor is too. When Betty feels that she understands Victor's issues, feelings, and concerns she will move to the next stage and get him to think outside his conflict zone, and then encourage him to agree to a joint meeting.

What emerges from the conversation with Victor is that the incident in the office after the missed site meeting was a pivotal point. This turned what for Victor was already a nagging doubt about Bryan into sense of complete mistrust. He was already "miffed that he did not get the job, and that someone fresh out of management school was deciding his schedule." He had missed the site meeting because he had been across the country, delayed on another site by some unexpected technical difficulties. He had tried to phone, but had been in a notoriously poor mobile signal area. So he decided to head into the office to make his apologies and catch up. He would, of course, have contacted the key people at the missed site meeting as soon as he could.

When he arrived at the office Bryan was seething and gave him no chance to explain or apologize. Victor had had to stand for 10 minutes being lectured, as colleagues walked past the office rather than coming in. His version of the conversation across the desk contained strong anger, embarrassment, and hurt. All that came across that day, he agrees, was anger. He had reacted to Bryan's lecture by telling him that he "had better things to do than be spoken to like he was a kid," and had walked out. He agrees that he has never really talked to Bryan about the embarrassment and hurt, only the anger.

Betty listens, acknowledges, and reflects. As is often the case, Victor feels that at least there is someone here who is not treating him as the demon in this situation. Betty is not on his side, but she is also not against him. She has the potential, in Victor's eyes, to be the bridge between his hurt and embarrassment and Bryan. This mediating manager has also become a possible way forward for Bryan, who is frustrated and cannot understand why Victor is so hostile. Betty has managed to demonstrate her impartiality by using the mediation process in a balanced, fair way, and by establishing rapport without taking sides.

Toward the end of the session with Victor Betty explains how a joint meeting would work. "When we meet, I will organize a neutral venue where you will both feel comfortable, and you will each get some time to put your points of view across without interruption. Once we are clear what the issues are, I will ask each of you to identify where you want to focus and we will then seek ways forward. As conversations like this can sometimes be heated or difficult I will help you keep the communication honest and open, but also manageable for both of you."

The benefits of mediation for Victor are:

- *Victor is keen to go ahead, as he feels that Bryan has misunderstood him and that this would be a chance to set the record straight.*
- *Like Bryan, he also thinks that communication could be improved and that Betty will help them structure their exchanges.*
- *Victor's sense of hurt and embarrassment may not be expressed directly at the joint session, but he is determined to let Bryan know how the incident after the missed site meeting has affected him. Victor is not out to get Bryan, but he has not been able to put that across before.*
- *The privacy of mediation and confidentiality convinces Victor that this will be a safe way of moving forward. He thinks it is unlikely to make the situation worse.*

KEY LEARNING POINTS
IMPARTIALITY

- The willingness to accept difficult feedback and challenges to the mediation process is a fundamental ingredient of impartiality. We have frequently observed mediators who announce their neutrality with pride then become defensive, or steamroller the parties when they demonstrate any fears about, or hostility to, mediation.
- Remember to balance descriptions of the process, e.g., "You will both be asked to contribute possible solutions."
- The stages of the mediation process are the anchor of your impartiality. Effective mediators ensure that each party gets full exposure to each stage. For example, if one party is reluctant to contribute ideas, do not simply accept this but find other ways of drawing them out. If the other party dominates, gently rein them back and make sure that you do not always initiate conversations with them.
- Impartiality is about what you do, not what you think or feel. It is possible to demonstrate impartiality even when, say, you dislike someone or, conversely, you are strongly attracted to someone and their experience.

Victor and Bryan agree to meet in a joint mediation session on neutral territory the next day. At the end of each session with them, some important closing tasks are set:

Bryan's issues
- *Victor does not allow himself to be managed effectively by Bryan.*
- *Victor is disrespectful.*
- *Victor has been undermining Bryan's status with the team.*

Victor's issues
- *Bryan smothers Victor.*
- *Bryan does not use Victor's experience and skills.*
- *Bryan has been clumsy in his communication.*

CHECKLIST
CLOSING AT THE END OF SEPARATE SESSIONS

- Let each party know that the sessions are confidential. It can be useful to agree a brief synopsis of issues from each party, which can be disclosed to the other should they need some sort of preview of issues before joining in with mediation.
- Keep the parties informed about the status and progress of the mediation, e.g., Bryan needs to be told that Victor has agreed and that a mutually acceptable date and venue have been set.
- Agree final brief summaries of the issues with the parties.

REFERENCES

1 Mulholland, J (1991) *The Language of Negotiation*, Routledge, London.
2 Fisher, R & Ury, W (1982) *Getting to Yes: Negotiating Agreement without Giving in*, Hutchinson, London.

6

A Joint Mediation Session

This chapter covers three more stages of the mediation process in detail:

- Stage 3: Assessment and setting up a joint meeting.
- Stage 4: Setting the scene and hearing the issues.
- Stage 5: Exploring and working on the issues.

The skills outlined in the previous chapter continue to be used throughout the face-to-face meetings, but some additional skills come into play when working with both parties together.

STAGE 3: ASSESSMENT AND SETTING UP A JOINT MEETING

Table 9 Stage 3: Assessment and setting up a joint meeting

Aims	Core skills
■ To get the parties to the joint meeting at a mutually convenient time and place.	1 Preparing the parties.
■ To help parties prepare appropriately.	2 Preparing the venue.
■ To hold the meeting and build commitment to the process if necessary.	
■ To get yourself ready for the task ahead.	

THE CONCEPT

Effective preparation contributes to the disputants' onward journey beyond conflict. Bad preparation will have a cost, particularly in those situations where anxiety and aggression are high and the commitment to mediation is on a knife edge.

THE SKILL

As Chapter 5 showed, mediating managers work hard to ensure that separate sessions are valuable in their own right, but also build toward the notion of direct partnership in a joint mediation meeting. Sometimes the individual sessions really free the conflict up, by allowing feelings to be vented and encouraging reflection. As a result, the two warring factions may feel less hostile and sort the problem out themselves without too much heat or pain. Mediation has to be voluntary for it to be fully effective, so be prepared to be disappointed occasionally when people refuse to make the most of it.

Once they have agreed to meet, the parties sometimes get cold feet or lose the commitment they built up with the mediator. Under these circumstances stay positive, keep listening to their concerns, and encourage them to get to the joint session. Emphasize the potential for early settlement that mediation offers. If they will not meet, you have four options:

- Close the process as constructively as possible, teasing out important learning and new information gained, and see whether it might be possible to construct some groundrules for the parties for future communication.
- Accept the decision, but leave the door open for mediation should their decision change.
- Withdraw the offer of mediation if it is no longer feasible.
- Offer "shuttle mediation" or side meetings during which the mediation process continues with the parties in separate rooms.

Confidentiality dictates that the mediator should not report their opinion about why the mediation stopped, merely the fact that it did.

■ Those who agree to come need arrangements for the meeting to be concluded speedily, efficiently, and painlessly, since it is important not to lose the momentum. So double check that people know where, when, and for how long the session will take place, and see that they get whatever clearance they need to attend.

■ Encourage the parties to think about what issues they will raise and how they will do so. They may also like to consider priorities, and to think ahead about a wide range of settlement options, if possible.

Preparing people who have agreed to attend

CORE SKILL 2: PREPARING THE VENUE

Before the meeting the mediator needs to spend time preparing the room where it will take place. The venue should be neutral, accessible, and as comfortable as possible. If it is a training or meeting room, check who else is booked in, in order to avoid awkward chance meetings. Imagine the parties' horror if they agreed to a private session with the mediator, then turned up at the location to find half their peers attending a training session next door.

THE CONCEPT

Organize the chairs so that they are in a non-confrontational layout and everyone has a good line of sight to the mediator and to one another. Set the chairs so that people can hear without feeling too close to each other. We recommend a Y shape of chairs without a table if possible, with the mediator sitting at the stem of the Y, and the parties half toward one another and the mediator. This is less adversarial and more encouraging of dialogue than is sitting across a desk. Round tables are better if you, or the parties, feel more comfortable with a table.

THE SKILL

Manage the reception area so it also suggests calm. Do not underestimate the power of a positive, balanced environment. Anyone who has ever waited for a doctor in a crowded waiting room full of people with hacking coughs, sitting on uncomfortable chairs, will tell you how much more unhealthy they suddenly feel.

We remember turning up at one venue and being asked to mediate at the end of a 25-seater boardroom table in a council debating chamber. Serried ranks of dignitaries peered down from gold-framed photos. We had told the parties that it would be an informal meeting. An agreement was reached, but only after we had abandoned the room and held the meeting in the adjoining cloakroom, among the Victorian porcelain. At another luxurious venue, we had met the parties in a comfortable vestibule and taken them into a well-decorated perfectly sized room, when one of the parties suddenly noticed a sign outside that we had missed: "Warning! High voltage! Keep away!" Fortunately the parties saw the funny side and we could not have asked for a better ice breaker. So take charge of your surroundings—or they will take charge of you.

Brief receptionists about who is coming and stress that it is for a private meeting. Check the building's policy on smoking and communicate it to all parties. Organize paper and pencils for notes, a flipchart if appropriate, and resources such as agreement forms and feedback forms as agreed (see Appendices for materials). Consider the parties' and mediator's special needs such as medication, refreshments, interpreters, transport to and from the venue, and so on.

Betty lets Bryan know that Victor is willing to meet early the next day. Bryan tries to tease out Betty's impression of Victor: "He's so arrogant isn't he? Can you see what I was saying?"

Betty respectfully tells Bryan that she cannot comment, just as she would not comment if anybody else asked her for her views.

Betty has checked some times and dates with Victor, and does the same with Bryan. She goes straight to their line manager to request that they be given time to attend, without being drawn into a conversation about what has gone on so far and how optimistic she is feeling, a conversation the line manager is certainly fishing for. She quickly establishes a two-hour appointment in two days' time, in a meeting room in another department. She emails both to confirm arrangements, sends a copy of the groundrules (see checklist below) and gives directions to the room, then phones them on the day to remind them again.

Betty has only made minimal notes, which she checked back with Bryan and Victor at the time for accuracy. These capture the key issues, any ideas about ways forward, and particular con-

cerns about mediation that the parties may have had. All of these will be useful reminders that will help Betty to manage her role and the meeting. Notes act as an aide memoire in mediation, not a formal record. The basic closing administrative tasks including recording are listed on page 223.

When Betty arrives 15 minutes early Victor is already outside the room, so she welcomes him and asks him to take a chair outside or come back in 15 minutes. She has to make sure that the room is set up as she had asked. On entering the room she finds that some equipment has been left out, so she arranges for that to be cleared, resets the chairs, and puts a welcome note on the flipchart. By now Bryan has arrived and Victor has disappeared. Betty greets Bryan, goes into the room with the door open, but does not invite Bryan in until Victor returns at the agreed starting time.

STAGES 4 AND 5: SETTING THE SCENE, EXPLORING AND WORKING ON THE ISSUES

Table 10 Stages 4 and 5

Stage 4: Setting the scene and hearing the issues

Aims

- To establish a safe, constructive environment.
- To encourage participation.
- To get the parties to **reflect** one at a time in their different ways on:
  - What has happened.
  - How they are feeling.
  - Their key concerns and issues.
  - How to move forward.

Core skills

1 Conversation management.
2 Setting the scene and building rapport.
3 Structuring the interaction.
4 Controlling the interaction.

Stage 5: Exploring and working on the issues

Aims

The process now moves gently into a more interactive phase. Until now communication has largely been through the mediator. Now the parties are invited to have a **limited exchange** of:

- Ideas.
- Feelings.
- Information.
- Understanding.

Core skills

5 Facilitation:
  - Framing issues constructively.
  - Highlighting common ground.
  - Encouraging low-risk exchange of information.
  - Agreeing the agenda.

THE CONCEPT

A "conversation is a complex interaction between two or more persons. Each participant and his or her behaviour, both verbal and non-verbal, can, and will, affect the behaviour of the other(s) within the conversational situation." Eric Shepherd first used the term "conversation management" in 1983, when training constables in the City of London Police. It is based on the notion that "it is imperative to understand how and why certain conversational behaviours will affect the other participants in the interaction." Investigative interviewing is a conversation with a clear purpose, and Dr Shepherd designed an approach that aimed to create consistent, ethical interviews that also produced useful outputs, such as information, background, and new awareness.[1]

The purpose of mediation is very different, but the notion of conversation management is still relevant, as it is important for mediators to think about how they are going to manage their own verbal and non-verbal behavior and the behavior of the parties.

THE SKILL

Managing their own behavior

As shown in Chapter 5, the mediator's behavior in the individual sessions is broadly non-directive. Once the general map of the process is set, a considerable amount of control is handed to the parties, who select and describe the content they wish to cover. The middle section of the separate sessions involves more action from the mediator, but still in very non-directive mode. Coaxing and coaching, the mediator seeks to draw the parties from descriptive to reflective conversation, stepping back and thinking about what they might want and how to move forward. When describing mediation toward the end of the session, the mediator will take a more active role, giving information, responding to questions and challenges, using influence and persuasion to move to the next stage.

The conversations created in the separate sessions provide the platform for the guided journey from conflict to cooperation that occurs in a joint mediation session. To help the parties have progressive conversations, the following qualities are useful during both separate and joint sessions:

- **Sensory acuity**—noticing changes and responses in another person during the communication process.
- **Flexibility**—the ability to adjust your behavior to changes that you notice in yourself and in others.
- **Congruence**—a state when you are functioning in such a way that what you say matches your behavior and how you feel inside. The opposite of this is polarity, when your behavior is indicative of strong differences in feeling and attitude, such as a desire to be forgiving but also a desire for revenge.

There are a number of aspects of conversational behavior that may well have become unproductive in a conflict situation. These will require management by the mediator if forward movement is to be achieved. A few examples will suffice.

Managing the behavior of the parties

- **Turn taking**—socialization, perceptions of status, and personal experience influence our perception of turn taking, e.g., who starts, who follows, who holds the floor, and how they cede that position. Mediation seeks equality of opportunity in turn taking in order to ensure that people get a chance to start and follow, initiate and respond, and are given equal access to the "floor." Mediators frequently invite parties to wait a turn or, conversely, invite people in. Consequently, everyone gets an opportunity to take their turn, in all stages of the process.
- **Topic control**—in negative conflicts battles often occur over which subjects require attention, and when and how the topic is changed. People introduce extra topics as diversions and work with several topics at once, in order to complicate rather than cooperate. Interactive mediators work with the parties to identify, sort, and prioritize topics. They also frequently keep the focus on a topic even when it is becoming difficult. "One issue at a time" is a phrase regularly utilized in mediation.
- **Type of listening required**—mishearing and not listening are common conflict conversational behaviors. Mediators are seeking to influence the parties toward active listening, and will frequently check with the parties to see what they

have heard, transmit information between them, and encourage detailed questioning of one another.

CORE SKILL 2: SETTING THE SCENE AND BUILDING RAPPORT

THE CONCEPT

The mediator will be the first person to speak during the joint session. Ensure that the opening part of the meeting is not merely a lecture but involves some communication. Parties will be nervous and may not be listening well to the mediator. Acknowledge that they may find this a lot to take in but that it does help in the long run. Remind them that they will be starting very soon.

During the statement be as positive as you can ("You have both taken a positive step in being here, and I will do everything I can to maximize your chances of leaving here feeling better than when you came in") and be friendly as well as authoritative.

THE SKILL

In order to model fairness and encourage participation:

- Maintain good eye contact and open body language with both parties.
- Ensure that you build rapport equally.
- Avoid any behavior that may demonstrate bias.
- Explain to both the overall purpose of the meeting.
- When seeking to check that people understand the process, direct questions to both parties.
- Invite questions about the process from both parties.
- Avoid being abrupt or judgmental if one party interrupts a great deal or is upset or withdrawn.
- Get through your introduction calmly and with as much confidence as you can muster.

The following checklists will help you to prepare your own opening mediator statement.

CHECKLIST
OPENING MEDIATOR STATEMENT

- Be positive, friendly, and assertive.
- Break the information into manageable chunks.
- Use clear language and avoid jargon.
- Pause regularly and check understanding, asking for questions.
- Check with each disputant by name about their willingness to participate and their agreement to groundrules.

CHECKLIST
MEDIATOR'S ROLES AND RESPONSIBILITIES

- **Fairness**—give each side the opportunity to speak and be heard, and work toward mutually acceptable resolutions.
- **Control**—control the session with the parties' help.
- **Non-judgmental**—it is the mediator's aim to respect all views, not take sides or judge which person, position, or solution is right/wrong.
- **Decision making**—the parties make the decisions, not the mediator.
- **Future focus**—help people work toward the future rather than go back continually over the past.
- **Make use of the time**—help the parties work at their own pace and make the best possible use of the time.
- **Confidentiality**—the mediator will not pass on anything they hear (there may be "riders" around issues of child abuse, criminal activity etc.).

CHECKLIST 3
GROUNDRULES

- **Be open**—about what is bothering you and what you need.
- **Be specific**—about what you want to happen, what you can do, and what you would like the other people involved to do.
- **Be patient**—people are asked to stay in the room and you can call a break to discuss problems and doubts if they arise.

- **Be focused**—talk about what you want and need, rather than giving your opinions about the other person.
- **Confidentiality**—keep whatever is discussed private: Notes will be destroyed, things said in mediation cannot be used in court or any other dispute-resolution process.
- **Listening**—listen to what the other people involved have to say.
- **Be non-threatening**—speak and behave in a non-threatening way; think how you yourself would like to be treated.

Signposting the session

Signposting helps people trust the mediator and participate fully. Although the parties are often keen to move on speedily with their dispute, they may still have reservations about the mediator, particularly if you are a manager they know or about whom they have heard rumors. The opening statement not only signposts the mediation process and where it is heading, but also dissipates fears about the mediator. It also demonstrates the mediator's intention to be fair and transparent and to disclose information about the process equally to all the parties.

Conclude the introduction by giving information about comfort facilities and breaks, clarifying the duration of the session, then outlining briefly the way it works:

"First, each of you will get a chance to put across a summary of your issues, feelings, and concerns without interruption. I will check that I have understood, then help clarify what you wish to focus on. We will then take the issues one by one and encourage more detailed discussion, with a view to identifying ways forward. Let me know if you start to find the process difficult or need a break. I will help you keep track of time and do my best to help you get the maximum out of the session. Any questions?"

CORE SKILL 3: STRUCTURING THE INTERACTION

THE CONCEPT

Structure in a conversation is reassuring when it is understood, serves the needs of the participants, and leads somewhere. It is alienating when it is imposed without explanation or as a substitute for action. In mediation, structure is the parties' and the mediator's friend. It is their road map toward progress. Conversely, it can also show how far people are away from their destination and what they need to do to get there. It helps them engage with one another and reduces misunderstandings.

The opening phase of a joint mediation session when you are setting the scene and hearing the issues is the most obviously structured part of the whole process. It follows a predetermined set of moves through to the final outcome, a summary of all the issues on the table by the mediator. The significance and purpose of each part of the process are signposted so that there can be no misunderstanding about what is going on and what is required of the parties. Each step is designed to hold the parties in a reflective, purposeful dialogue, and to resist all attempts by them either to resolve the conflict too early, or to slip back into the negative habits that have defined their dispute so far.

The interactive mediator uses a number of behaviors to sustain a structured interaction, as follows.

THE SKILL

Facilitated sequential activity

Externally facilitated sequential activity has real value in a conflict, as it encourages the disputants to step out of, and finally abandon, their own failing notions of appropriate sequencing. In the early phases of mediation the sequence is predetermined and designed to initiate discussion without resurrecting the conflict's existing dynamic. People participate quite willingly in the sequence, particularly if they know what is coming and why, and can see the benefits. (This is why it is so important to make it clear to the parties in separate sessions what the joint meeting is all about and how it works.) Sequence is a comforting, reassuring quality in interactions when it is mutually agreed and fairly managed. The mediator will keep an eye on turn taking to ensure that there are opportunities for everyone to participate.

Stage 4 of the mediation process, *Setting the scene and hearing the issues*, follows a standard sequence, which is designed to model fairness and consistency. This sequence prevails no matter what occurs.

```
┌─────────────────────────────────────────────────────────┐
│                     CHECKLIST                             │
│               SEQUENCE FOR STAGE 4                        │
│                                                           │
│  1  Welcome and words of encouragement.                  │
│  2  Personal introductions: Check what the parties prefer │
│     to be called, now that they are in the room together. │
│  3  Brief explanation of the purpose of the mediation and │
│     the role of the mediator.                             │
│  4  Introduce and agree groundrules and what is expected  │
│     from the parties.                                     │
│  5  You may find it useful to have the groundrules on a   │
│     flipchart. You could also give them to the parties on │
│     a card, which they could read while they are waiting  │
│     for the session to start.                             │
│  6  Explain how the session will be run.                  │
│  7  Invite one party to speak while the other listens and │
│     does not interrupt.                                   │
│  8  The mediator summarizes this version.                 │
│  9  Invite the other party to speak while the other       │
│     listens and does not interrupt.                       │
│ 10  The mediator summarizes this version.                 │
└─────────────────────────────────────────────────────────┘
```

Pacing and timing

The mediator monitors parties' contributions, initiates discussion of time boundaries, and manages these boundaries with the parties. Interactive mediators work at a pace that matches the parties' needs, checking often that people are keeping up or not rushing ahead.

Encouraging a mixture of speaking and listening

One person has to go first, but each party will get a short period of time to speak and to listen. Early on, the mediator allocates time for an initial statement by each of the parties (up to 10 minutes each) and expects all parties to remain attentive and not to interrupt while the other is speaking. Later in the process, when the structure of a dialogue is less well defined, mediators will be seen to be helping those who may have listened for a long time to respond, and those who have been talking for a long while to listen.

Directing

While they are getting used to the process and the mediator, the parties are asked to speak through the mediator. As the process unfolds they speak more and more directly to one another. Eventually they will be speaking to one another while the mediator watches and listens.

Betty opens the work for the disputants with an invitation for Bryan to express his core issues in 10 minutes, while Victor listens. She nominates Bryan and, as she explains, "Part of my role as mediator is to decide who goes first, and I have chosen Bryan today." She may attract criticism from Victor for this, but explains that he will get his chance and that her choice was purely procedural not personal.

Once Bryan's uninterrupted time is complete, Betty summarizes. She then invites Victor to outline his issues. Victor has been sitting on a couple of what he sees as vital points. He wants to use his time to outline in detail his version of a couple of crucial events: the missed site meeting, and a later staff meeting to which Bryan had alluded. Betty explains that he will get a chance to respond fully later, but for now it is better for him and Bryan if he outlines his own issues. Having reserved this piece of work for later, Betty must ensure that she returns to it, or Victor will start to think that the structure is running against him.

Eventually Victor highlights his concerns, but while Betty is summarizing, Bryan suggests that he could take a break as he has heard it all before. Betty requests he stays so that all three of them can be clear about the issues registered so far. She also raises the issue of parity. Since Victor heard the mediator's summary of Bryan's issues, she would like Bryan, in return, to abide by the same convention.

CORE SKILL 4: CONTROLLING THE INTERACTION

THE CONCEPT

Chapter 7 deals with conflict management, particularly handling anger, upset, and aggression. In almost all mediations a moment soon arises when the mediator will need to exercise some control, to ensure that the interaction is fair, balanced, and as respectful as possible. This section will help you understand the type of control that is most helpful at this stage.

These early exchanges set the scene for what happens later. The integrity of the structure outlined above should be maintained, as it forms the bridge into the more challenging part of the process. The purpose of control in mediation is to enable the process to happen, and to encourage the parties to participate fully in exploring their differences and moving forward.

Different situations present different challenges to mediators, and ideally you should be able to find a way of matching the response to the situation. Some people and situations require more direct control than others. There is a continuum of control strategies from the least to the most directive, as illustrated in Figure 5.

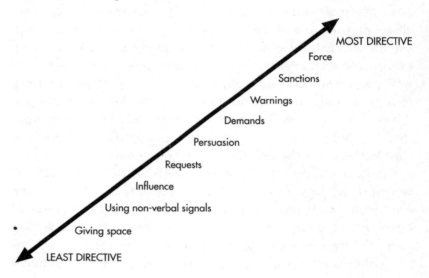

Figure 5 Continuum of control strategies

Mediators generally operate somewhere between giving space and persuasion. Rarely, if ever, should they be making demands, issuing warnings, or operating sanctions. Forcing is completely out of the question.

The control habits that some people develop associated with their role at work or in life generally may produce outcomes and often allow them to feel better about themselves. However, as mentioned above, control in mediation is exercised in order to sustain a constructive conversation and in partnership with the parties.

There are four key principles of control in interactive mediation. Control should be exercised in a way that is:

- **Balanced**—fair, even-handed, and consistent.
- **Step by step**—structured, moving from less directive to directive, as appropriate.
- **Empathetic**—showing understanding and acknowledging people's right to their feelings.
- **Motivational**—encouraging and non-blaming.

When mediators believe that they may need to exercise some control, some key questions have to be asked:

THE SKILL

What is my need for control telling me about myself? Am I uncomfortable with what is going on? The mediating manager's aim must be to exercise control so that the parties can continue to participate and allow the process to happen. Therefore we need to:

How is what is going on affecting me?

- Keep a clear focus on the parties' behavior.
- Monitor our own response and keep it under control.
- Monitor the parties' responses to one another and intervene appropriately.

Mediators also need to consider where in the mediation process they and the parties are. For example, when the parties are in uninterrupted time, the mediators would need to cut interruptions short and only allow one person to speak. Later on, when exchange is desirable, for example as issues are being discussed and options generated, mediators should be careful not to overcontrol the parties, since some conflict is both useful and necessary prior to resolution. For example:

Where are we in the mediation process?

- This may be the first time that parties have spoken directly to each other for a very long while and they may need to clear the air.
- This may be the only way in which parties can initially communicate.
- Parties may be exchanging information that is new and

relevant to their dispute, albeit in an angry way.
■ This may be a normal, acceptable way for these parties to communicate.

What is the appropriate response to the situation?

Mediators seek to match their interventions to the situation in front of them. If it is fierce keep it firm, if it is going keep it flowing (see below). Once stages 4 and 5 have passed, free interchange is helpful and the mediator is less obviously structuring the interaction. Here interruptions for control will often be less frequent.

Difficult situations merit different responses. Look at the two common situations in the opening phase of the Bryan and Victor joint mediation session. How would you have responded? Would your response have measured up to the criteria above? We will take you through some inappropriate control methods and then highlight how Betty, the mediating manager, responds.

Bryan looks uncomfortable as the mediator introduces the session and petulantly moves a chair back a couple of feet. When Betty catches his eye he interrupts, saying, "Can't we bloody get on with it?"

"Bad mediator" response—what you might really like to say

(Mediator wrinkles brow and frowns) "Just let me finish, if you don't mind. We'll get going in good time. It's really important that you hear me out" (haughty) or "I thought you were going to be trouble. No, only joking" (over-matey and sarcastic) or "Look, I'm only doing my job" (defensive).

Mediating manager's response

The mediating manager's response increases in directiveness:

■ *Betty merely holds eye contact and pauses, to see if Bryan has any more to say. Then she continues with her introduction. If Bryan still seems frustrated and verbalizes this again, she moves on:*
■ *"I hear you'd like to get on but bear with me a little longer. I am nearly finished" (acknowledging frustration and negotiating more time). If Bryan still looks impatient and interrupts again, she moves on:*
■ *"Thanks Bryan, I can see your frustration but I need to finish the introduction. It is an important part of the mediation and will help you in the long run" (acknowledgment and using*

influence skills and persuasion to suggest behavioral change).

As another example, Bryan begins his uninterrupted time and before long refers to Victor as "arrogant" and "pig-headed." Victor interrupts: "That's simply not true, Bryan." To the mediator: "You're not going to let him get away with that, are you?"

"It's up to Bryan what he says. Just listen, Victor" (lacking impartiality) or "Carry on Bryan" (avoidance) or "Don't worry Victor, you can get your own back in a minute" (provocative).

The "bad mediator" response

- *Initial balanced response: "You will get your chance to respond, Victor. Bryan, I wonder if you could give specific examples of what Victor does that affects you?" If the interruptions continue:*
- *"You've clearly got a lot to say, Victor, and you will get your time shortly" (acknowledging and motivating to exercise some self-discipline). If Bryan persists in using general comments about Victor:*
- *"Bryan, when you say 'arrogant,' what do you base that on? How is that affecting you?" (requesting less personalized behavior and concentrating on what Bryan is actually experiencing rather than merely his perception of Victor). If they both continue to spark off one another:*
- *"Bryan and Victor, I can see this is difficult for you, but don't forget why you came here, to see if you could talk these issues through. This is just the initial exploratory stage. If you could concentrate on specifics, Bryan, and you could listen without interrupting for a while longer, Victor, we should be able to move on" (using influence and persuasion, encouraging self-discipline, and reminding them of their aims, then specifically requesting some changes in behavior).*

Mediating manager's response

Betty maintains the parameters of the process and the conversation in the mediation room does not become destructive. When Victor talks through his issues he initially responds to Bryan's comments. Betty draws him on to his own issues through gentle prompting and guiding, and after a couple of interruptions Bryan remains silent, in listening mode. The end product of this part of the process is a joint summary of the issues raised, which Betty writes on the flipchart with the parties' permission.

Bryan's issues
- Victor does not allow himself to be managed effectively by Bryan.
- Victor is disrespectful.
- Victor has been undermining Bryan's status with the team.

Victor's issues
- Bryan smothers Victor.
- Bryan does not use Victor's experience and skills.
- Bryan has been clumsy in his communication.

CORE SKILL 5: FACILITATION

THE CONCEPT

To facilitate literally means to make things easier. Facilitation skills are particularly useful when parties are finding it difficult to communicate, negotiate, or move forward.

Table 11 What facilitation offers the parties and the process

Confidence	Direction	Tone	Overview	Sense of progress
Giving energy and momentum: "You can do this!" "It is quite normal to feel that way at this stage."	Choosing productive approaches to the task; setting groundrules; keeping discussion on track; handling disruption.	Creating an atmosphere that encourages respectful, non-judgmental attitudes and helping participants deal with difficult, unpleasant, or discouraging moments.	Helping people look at each part of the problem; at each point of view; at the past, present, and future situation. Reminding them of what they came for.	Reminding people of what they have already accomplished; building morale; contradicting a feeling of "we're getting nowhere."

THE SKILLS

After the mediator's joint summary and uninterrupted time, the mediation moves from reflection into limited exchange, and at this point things usually get tougher. There are four basic facilitation skills that will help people manage to exchange information, views, feelings, and concerns more effectively:

■ Framing issues constructively.
■ Highlighting common ground.
■ Encouraging low-risk exchange of information.
■ Agreeing the agenda.

Interactive mediators help people discuss issues effectively by framing them in a way that is specific, non-blaming, and if possible of mutual interest.

Framing issues constructively

Bryan frequently refers to Victor as "difficult," "resentful," or "not willing to be managed." Once uninterrupted time and the combined issues summary are finished, Betty seeks to clarify the issue: "So what is it that is making it difficult for you to manage Victor?"

"He doesn't listen, and is openly dismissive of me in staff meetings. Also you can never get hold of him when you need him."

Victor disagrees at this point, but Betty encourages him to pause and clarifies: "So your issue is about how Victor communicates with you, particularly his listening and what you believe is a dismissive approach in staff meetings and the fact that he has, in your experience, been difficult to contact at times."

Bryan concurs.

Victor reiterates, "You, Bryan, are the worst communicator in the world. Sometimes no one in the team has a clue what you are on about."

Betty reframes the issue: "Victor, you also have concerns about Bryan's communication."

Although people in disputes may be openly hostile they often share issues, albeit coming at them from a different direction. People in a conflict often only notice their differences, so highlighting common ground can set a more positive tone and reduce the sense of separation between the parties.

Highlighting common ground

*Betty detects several areas of common ground in the two sepa-
rate accounts of events:*

- *Both Bryan and Victor agree that their relationship did not
  get off to a good start, and that they have not felt comfortable with one another since then.*
- *They are both aware that this conflict has been spilling out
  into the team.*
- *Both agree that the situation needs to be resolved.*
- *Both are aware that there is pressure to perform, as staff
  numbers have been reduced.*

**Encouraging low-risk exchange
of information**

Exchange of low-risk information helps the mediator and the
parties take a break from the conflict and talk about something
they both know and understand, in relation to their own work
area. This low-risk exchange will also fill in some very useful
background, as it focuses on areas that seem to be contributing to the conflict.

*Although Betty is a senior manager, she is not familiar with the
workings of Bryan and Victor's team. She asks both to talk
through their work areas and what projects they are currently
working on. Her request is accompanied by an instruction not to
touch directly on areas in contention.*

*Betty has a hunch that they perceive communication conven-
tions differently, particularly how the open-plan office affects
communication. She checks this out: "What experience have
you of working in an open-plan office? Do you like it? What do
you need from your colleagues in that space?" She discovers
that Victor thinks lively conversations in the open-plan office are
fine. It has been like that for years. Bryan is new to this environment, having come from a job where he had his own office.
He prefers a more subdued atmosphere in public areas.*

Agreeing the agenda

*The limited exchange of stage 5 of mediation can be heated,
but Bryan and Victor get through fairly quietly. They are thanked
by Betty for their contributions and then asked to help her create
a checklist of items to be discussed. Bryan wants to concentrate
on his managerial relationship with Victor. Victor does not see*

this as a problem, but also wants to cover what he needs from a manager in that slot. As this is an issue for both of them, it will probably be the first to be discussed. Victor is keen to go back over the events before and after the site meeting and clarify how he feels. Bryan is not keen, but is prepared to have a look at that again if they can first take care of the managerial issue.

In this case agenda setting is relatively straightforward. It is not always as easy, since parties sometimes wish to introduce and discuss ideas that may not be suitable. This is covered in Chapter 8.

REFERENCE

1 Information on conversation management taken from Milne, R & Bull, R (2000) *Investigative Interviewing Psychology and Practice*, Wiley, Chichester.

7

Moving On

For many interactive mediators stage 6—building agreements and relationships—is the most exacting, but also the most exciting, part of the process. Until now the mediator has occupied a variety of roles: umpire, anchor, coach, and mentor. Each of these roles fits broadly into the leadership category, with the mediator being fairly visible and in control of the process.

In particularly hostile settings most of the conversation may have happened through the mediator, with limited direct eye contact or acknowledgment between the parties. At this stage it is common for parties to feel as though they are being restrained to a degree. From here on in, mediators seek to switch gear and encourage the parties to engage directly in a prolonged exchange, and the really dynamic work begins.

At this stage the parties are encouraged to achieve a number of difficult transitions. They are asked to move:

- From exchanging information, feelings and perceptions to defining issues and problems.
- From talking about what the problem is to exploring and exchanging solutions.
- From the past to the future.
- From talking through and to the mediator to prolonged direct conversation with one another.

Interactive mediators provide support of various types at this stage, but they also have some adjustments to make. Their way of working shifts:

- From being at the center of the process to being at the edge or in the background.
- From holding the parties back to encouraging them to move forward.
- From working in a clearly sequential manner to a more fluid, dynamic style.

STAGE 6: BUILDING AGREEMENTS AND RELATIONSHIPS; AND STAGE 7: CLOSURE

Table 12 Stages 6 and 7: Building agreements and relationships, and closure

Stage 6: Building agreements and relationships

Aims

- To create opportunities for forward movement.
- To support the parties through a number of transitions in the process.
- To continue full participation and sustain a safe environment.
- To achieve constructive exchange of:
  - Ideas.
  - Feelings.
  - Information.
  - Understanding.
  - Ways of moving forward.

Core skills

1 Creating a safe space for exchange of information, feelings, and perceptions.
2 Keeping it safe, keeping things moving.
3 Generating and assessing options.

Stage 7: Closure

Aims

- To capture the positive aspects that emerge from the discussion.
- To close as constructively as possible on the issues and the process.
- To encourage parties to move on toward a mutually acceptable outcome.
- Where that is not possible to move on to:
  - Consider what will happen next.
  - Create some groundrules for future interactions.

Core skills

4 Closing on the issues.
5 Firming up agreements.
6 Closing on the interaction and the process.

THE CONCEPT

Interactive mediators' conversation management and control techniques will be less obvious here. The parties are encouraged to speak directly to one another about the events that have brought them to this point. You never quite know what is coming next, so mediators need to remain calm, neutral, and attentive.

What we are looking for at this stage is a sense that the parties are starting to communicate, for example that there is some evidence of turn taking, listening, and fewer personalized comments. This shift is not immediately self-evident and the more constructive dialogue may take a while to emerge. The parties have the opportunity first to find their own way through conflict about the events, feelings, and perceptions that have caused the difficulties between them.

THE SKILL

The work already done by the mediating manager and the parties in the separate sessions and the early stages of the joint mediation session has by this stage built a degree of rapport and an atmosphere that is safer and less acrimonious than had been present in this conflict until now. The space now offered to the parties is something new, and there is a great deal that the mediator can do to create a safe space to help the parties feel confident enough to say what they need to, without utilizing destructive or defensive behavior.

- **Remind them briefly at the start of the aims of mediation**: "You came here because there were things you needed to say to one another, so try to get those ideas and issues across in a way that the other person can make sense of." "We're looking for clarity here, not for winners and losers." "It would really help if you spoke directly to one another now, about what you consider to be the key incidents, to try to build some understanding about what happened, how it affected you, and then what you want to do about it."
- **Maintain positive, open body language throughout**, paying equal attention to all parties.

- **Assess the parties' comfort levels and sense of progress** and if necessary **check** with them how they are feeling: "What sense do you have of how the discussion is going?" "Are you comfortable with that?" "You look and sound upset. Are you all right to continue?" "Is it OK for Victor to take a little more time, as long as you get a chance to reply?"
- **Reinforce positive behavior**. Give positive feedback to the parties, for example for keeping in conversation even when it becomes heated, for responding to one another, for conciliatory gestures: "Bryan says he did not realize that you had tried to contact him, Victor." "You recognize, Victor, that your frustration at not getting the manager's job had probably spilled over into the first team meeting."

When the parties take advantage of this space a different, more progressive type of conflict starts to emerge.

Bryan and Victor work in a fairly non-sequential way, talking about several issues at once, jumping ahead to problem solving although the problem is still not clear. But before long they refocus on the key issue and clarify exactly what their perception of the problem is. "So for you, Bryan, I became an enemy after that staff meeting." "Yes, and that's why I was keen to make my point after you had missed that site meeting. This has, I suppose, been a bit of a battle of wills."

Early on in their discussion about the angry exchange in the open-plan office, Bryan and Victor revert to more competitive turn taking. However, they manage this with phrases that sound hostile, but do achieve some genuine exchange, such as "Let me finish," "Would you mind not interrupting?" or "Can I get a word in now?"

Parties who are invited to speak directly to one another commonly adopt less active listening styles. They react to what they think they have heard, don't acknowledge one another, and often don't actually respond to the questions asked, but give answers to other, imaginary questions. This is probably familiar to them from previous conversations they have had about their conflict, before the mediation.

Victor keeps insisting that Bryan is criticizing the quality of his work and "maligning his professional integrity." This time, with no prompting, this accusation does not flare up. Bryan requests some better listening: "Did you actually hear what I said? I've never doubted your ability, or your integrity with the general public and our clients."

Victor also chastises Bryan when he does not answer a question about the now notorious argument in the open-plan office. "Bryan, did you get my message on your mobile? Did you give me a chance to put my side of the story?"

Bryan continues to say how aggressive Victor was. "No, you're not answering my question. I want to know! It's really important that you understand that I knew you were going to be upset and wanted to set matters right. But I wasn't given the chance."

This new, more constructive dialogue emerges for a number of reasons:

- The mediator is there.
- The space and time are set aside and the atmosphere is right.
- The confidentiality and the growing sense of rapport and safety of the setting give the parties permission they may not have had in other environments.
- The parties are feeling more positive about themselves and their ability to influence one another and the situation.
- There is an overriding sense of opportunity at this stage of the process, and people do not want to miss it.

Once this constructive conflict emerges, the interactive mediator's job is to:

- Offer space and pay attention.
- Listen and note down key pieces of information that emerge.
- Stay calm and avoid the temptation to do or say something.

When a phase of the conversation seems to be drawing to a close or running out of steam:

- Be positive and affirm the parties' efforts.
- Help them pull together information.
- If necessary recycle information to get them restarted—"So you said that you had some ideas about email etiquette. Can we get back to that?"
- Summarize what has been said and where people seem to be in the process.

CORE SKILL 2: KEEPING IT SAFE, KEEPING THINGS MOVING

THE CONCEPT

Not all disputes or disputants are ready by stage 6 to sustain a constructive conflict and move forward together. There are some core mediator behaviors that will help people maintain their participation and continue moving forward:

THE SKILLS

- Maintaining a non-judgmental, positive attitude.
- Continued structuring of the interaction.
- Highlighting movement through the process.
- Highlighting what is not in dispute.
- Clarifying perceptions and agreeing to differ.
- Discussing interests.

These behaviors are also very useful for difficult situations in general.

Maintaining a non-judgmental, positive attitude

Once the first issue is selected for discussion we are about a third of the way through the mediation process. There is still much to say about the past and many feelings to bring to the surface. Sometimes these spill out furiously and people's ability to maintain self-discipline and respect is tested to the full.

Do not allow yourself to get too depressed about this, or frustrated by the parties. It is perfectly normal at this stage. The chances are that the parties know you are there and feel safe enough to be open, and that productive thoughts and feelings will emerge. You watch and listen, and the parties know that they have a custodian of calm and positive energy to fall back on.

Victor starts to tell Bryan how bad he felt about missing the site meeting, even though the issue they decided to discuss is the managerial relationship. Bryan wants to start with the first diffi-cult incident for him, which was the first staff meeting, where he claims Victor was "hostile from the start."

They call Betty in to "make a judgment." She declines and puts the situation back to them, but is positive about what to them seem like conflicting demands: "I think it would be good to dis-cuss both situations so that you can each understand how the other felt. Perhaps you could both go through your version of events and describe how the situation left you feeling? I think each situation has had an effect on the managerial relationship."

Bryan says, "Typical of you mediators. Too weak to make a decision. Let Victor go first."

Betty responds briefly, "Thanks for that, Bryan. You are get-ting the hang of this."

Continued structuring of the interaction

- **Broadly mapping the sequence**—at the outset of this stage it is useful to suggest a continuing proposed struc-ture. To put it simply, as Betty did, "We are going to finish discussing what the problem is, and then move on to what the solutions might be."
- **Regulate the pacing with the parties**—if the mediator or the parties sense that things are moving too fast, a slow-down can be introduced, for example by asking for more information, summarizing what has already been said, or checking that people have understood what has been said so far.

If people are getting stuck in arguments about the past, acknowledge their need to get these things off their chests, seek guidance from them on when they will be ready to move to the future, and discuss what they would like to do to change things.

Highlighting movement through the process

When people are ready they sometimes move seamlessly from discussions about past events to the future.

Once Bryan and Victor agree that their relationship needs some work, they begin to make suggestions. "Why don't you actually set up an electronic diary for the whole team, rather than chas-ing us all for dates?" suggests Victor.

"Who's going to bloody well do that?" says Bryan.

Betty interrupts: "Hold on a moment, Bryan. I think it's really good that you are now both discussing ways forward. Let's get all the suggestions clear first before we respond to them. Do you have any ideas for how to address the contact and movement issue?"

One key contentious issue was Victor's feeling that Bryan was overmonitoring him, sending email after email with questions about what Victor was doing, technical issues, the current status of projects. As a result, he felt he was being smothered. Bryan eventually explained that the intention of the intensive contact was to get himself up to scratch with the agency's conventions by tapping into Victor's knowledge. What had been perceived as undermining and an attempt to get Victor to account for every move was in fact Bryan's way of making the most of his most senior member of staff.

Betty recognized this significant new understanding between them: "So in fact, Bryan, your intention was to pick up know-ledge speedily through Victor, but you never told him this. Victor, you saw this as intrusive. But now you can see its purpose. Bryan, we may need to come back at some other time to how managers should go about getting themselves technically up to speed. So how else do managers make the most of their experienced team members? How can you two work on this together?"

By this stage some issues are well defined, some points of fact agreed, some key incidents identified, and some feelings shared. There may also be some immovable features of the situation that cannot be changed. The interaction can be enhanced by bringing the less contentious areas to the fore. This has the effect of reducing the potential magnitude of the dispute to more manageable dimensions. It also prevents the parties from entering into prolonged conflict about these areas.

Highlighting what is not in dispute

Bryan and Victor agree that Victor missed the site meeting. They also agree that it made life difficult for both of them. Although Victor still has a sense of disappointment about it, he concedes that Bryan is, and will remain, the new manager of the team, not him. Bryan also acknowledges that Victor knows more than he does about the technical areas of their job. Victor is pleased to hear Bryan say that he does not have any reservations about Victor's ability to do his job well. Betty highlights these undisputed facts and statements, seeking to ring-fence them against future conflict. If other areas that are not in dispute emerge, Betty will almost certainly draw attention to them to keep building confidence.

Clarifying perceptions and
agreeing to differ

Sometimes people cannot agree about events or their assessment of issues. Conflict is often a matter of perception, but interactive mediators do not adjudicate, nor do they dismiss perceptions. They work with the parties to understand what people believe was going on, get the others involved to understand how the perception was formed and what it signified, and then move beyond perceptions to issues, sometimes agreeing to differ if necessary.

Bryan is upset by Victor's perception of him as "inexperienced and naïve as a manager." Betty encourages Victor to explain his reasons, then clarify how this affects the managerial issue, and what exactly he wants from Bryan. Bryan, too, gets a chance to describe how he sees Victor, and what he wants from Victor as a team member.

After discussing for some time their argument in the open-plan office following the missed site meeting, Victor and Bryan were finding it hard to understand or accept the other's interpretation of events. Victor thought that Bryan had been abrupt and patronizing, and that he had dominated the conversation. Bryan thought Victor had been defensive and refused to join in despite much prompting.

Betty says, "So you have different recollections of that meeting? This is hardly surprising, as you were both upset, and you agree that you needed to have a conversation about what had happened. What are the issues that this meeting raises?"

Bryan says, "It's about how he reacts to being managed by me."

Victor replies, "His management style is the issue. He doesn't listen."

The scene is now set to seek ways forward on the issue of creating an effective manager/team member relationship.

It is often useful to preface the generation of options by discussing interests. These can then be used later to evaluate options.

Discussing interests

Betty asks both disputants in turn: "So generally, what do you think would constitute effective management in a job like yours, and what would be expected from an experienced team member in how they relate to the manager?"

Bryan immediately replies, "Well, a manager should be allowed to manage."

Betty seeks examples of what this would look like.

Bryan comments, "He should be able to have access to all team members individually and be able to support and monitor them in their work. A new manager, particularly, should be allowed the space to bed in and find their own way."

Victor adds, "A manager should make the most of the experience in the team."

Betty can now ask a mutual interest question: "So how can we find a way forward that allows you to manage, Bryan, and you, Victor, to feel that your experience is being utilized?"

CORE SKILL 3: GENERATING AND ASSESSING OPTIONS

One of the strengths of interactive mediation is that it empowers the parties to make their own decisions, which are not imposed and draw from the parties' own experience and knowledge of their jobs and one another. Mediators assist in that process, but do not lead it. There are a number of potential pitfalls that must be avoided by mediators at this point:

THE CONCEPT

- The mediator thinks of a great idea and suggests it. One party likes it, the other does not and your impartiality is gone.
- The process is often slower at this point than it would be if the mediator was directly contributing to option generation,

so there is a temptation for the mediator to become frustrated.

■ Some ideas could seem unworkable and may be dismissed by the mediator too early.

■ The parties ask the mediator to make suggestions (but of course there is no guarantee that they will like them or abide by them).

■ The parties ask the mediator to give an opinion on the options so far discussed.

THE SKILL

Ask, offer, or trade

There is a systematic way of helping parties generate options. Ask all three questions of party A before moving to party B. Ask party B not to comment on party A's ideas until the close of this dynamic. Be clear that you will work through all issues in this way.

■ To party A: "What would you ask from party B on your first issue?"

■ To party A: "What can you offer to do for party B on your first issue, to help them give you what you want on this issue?"

■ To party A: "What can you trade for B, in return for them giving you the solution you want on your first issue?"

■ To party B: "What can you offer on party A's first issue?"

■ To party B: "What can party A do for you, to help you give this on their first issue?"

■ To party B: "What do you ask in exchange on another issue, if you give in on party A's first issue?"

Now invite both parties to discuss the options that this sequence has generated. One golden rule about option generation is if party A suggests something and party B declines, ask party B to come up with an alternative.

If options are still hard to generate the following approaches can help:

Encouraging creative thinking about options

■ Summarize existing options and ask for one more idea.

■ Idea storming—collect all ideas without comment or criticism.

■ Take an incremental approach—what would be your first choice, second choice, third choice?

- Break larger problems down into smaller bits—rather than looking at how to make someone a better team member, collect ideas about support for them, improving communication, building awareness and skills.
- Circular questions—put yourself in other people's shoes, for example what do you think the other side would want you to do?
- Narrowing extreme positions—is there anything between the positions that you have suggested?
- "What if" questions—what might life be like if…?
- Get comparisons—in another similar situation, what would happen?

Parties get very quickly into assessing options—"No that won't work!" or "That will do then!"—before the options have been fully explored. Mediators need to slow the parties down so that they assess options fully and build on the positive parts of any ideas, rather than discarding them. Some parties find assessing options a straightforward process, with both sides working hard on testing proposals and modifying theirs when necessary, but if negotiations have been difficult the parties will probably want help from the mediators.

Victor and Bryan are not short of ideas. For Betty the problem is getting them to evaluate ideas and make decisions. She asks their permission to write on the flipchart the suggestions currently on the table for improving their working relationship. This is the list that is generated, using her notes and their memories:

- Electronic diary for better contact.
- One-to-one monthly meetings.
- Mobile messages checked daily, particularly before crunch meetings.
- No public arguments.
- Charm school for Victor.
- Technical briefing sessions by Victor for Bryan.
- Team away day.
- Cast-iron guarantee from Victor never to miss another important site meeting.

Assessing options

It may well be that some more can be added. There are a number of ways in which Betty can help assess the options:

Role of the mediator in
assessing options

■ ***Ranking options****—"So are any of these ideas definitely 'out' as far as you are concerned, definitely 'worth discussing' or 'maybe'?" Then concentrating on areas of consensus: "You both agree that 'no public arguments' is a good idea and that 'charm school for Victor' was meant as a joke." Another ranking approach is helping parties to look at their first choice, second choice, and third choice.*

■ ***Reality testing****—will this work? Or in this case: "No public arguments—how will that work? What will you do, where will you go, if you do need to have an urgent, potentially difficult conversation?"*

■ ***Probing****—does this satisfy people's interests? "You mentioned, Bryan, that you wanted to tap into Victor's technical expertise. Will briefing sessions achieve this for you?" Focus on the benefits of settling or not settling.*

■ ***Encouraging exploration and explanation of options****—"You were not keen on the idea of an electronic diary, Bryan, particularly the cost and the time taken setting it up. Perhaps you could give us your ideas on this?"*

■ ***Reminding people of their interests and using these to evaluate options****—"Victor, you said you were prepared to be managed, but not smothered. So would monthly one-to-ones work for you?" "Bryan, you said you wanted more access to Victor. Victor is suggesting every other month for one-to-ones. Will that do it, and if not what else could either of you suggest?"*

Eventually, of course, decisions have to be made. To ensure a fair process of discussion and decision, the mediator will often seek the parties' agreement to criteria for assessment that are fair and as objective as possible under the circumstances.

CHECKLIST
CRITERIA TO ASSESS OPTIONS

- Do they satisfy real, substantive interests, goals and objectives?
- Do they work in the long and/or short term?
- Has the process of arriving at a solution been fair and have all parties participated fully?
- Are options fair and just? Do they take into account what can legitimately be expected from each side?
- Do they promote a better relationship?
- Have all options that provide for a win/win solution been explored, before trading some win/lose options?

CORE SKILL 4: CLOSING ON THE ISSUES

There are two main forms of closure in mediation:

- As each issue reaches a conclusion.
- At the end of the session.

For mediators closure is primarily about stopping something, rounding ideas up, setting limits. It should be handled sensitively and, if necessary, firmly. Mediation cannot be an endless process. The fact that it is limited offers a real opportunity for focused, productive activity.

Closure does not always mean resolution. Whatever the circumstances, mediators should aim to achieve as constructive a closure as possible on the issues, the interaction, and the dispute-resolution process.

As the parties begin to make decisions about ways forward, the interactive mediator becomes the agent of reality. Conduct a reality test, check fall-back positions, and ensure that the parties know what they are agreeing to and what it involves. Do not forget that you are not the arbiter of reality.

The following activities assist in achieving constructive closure on the issues:

THE CONCEPT

THE SKILL

■ Summarize issues where agreements have been made.
■ Clarify what has been agreed and whether the parties want to construct a written agreement (see below for some tips).
■ Where issues are partly resolved, check what has already been agreed and what other work might need to be done (and how a follow-up session can be arranged).
■ Clarify issues that may not be decided in the time left and consider what to do about them.
■ Clarify the status of all issues and check that the parties agree and are clear about that.

CORE SKILL 5: FIRMING UP AGREEMENTS

THE CONCEPT

Written agreements have a practical and symbolic use. They are not legally binding, but are useful if parties want them, for confirming what has been agreed and recognizing the work they have done.

THE SKILL

An effective mediation agreement should:

■ Use clear and simple language.
■ Set times and be detailed.
■ Be practical, workable, and specific.
■ Include not just actions agreed, but all conciliatory moves and acknowledgments made by the parties throughout the mediation.
■ Be balanced, positive, and provide for the future.
■ Include fall-back arrangements, to be reviewed by all the parties.

CORE SKILL 6: CLOSING ON THE INTERACTION AND THE PROCESS

Interaction

■ Highlight useful information and learning that may have emerged.
■ Clarify the degree of confidentiality for these issues; some may need to be fed back to the team. Discuss this carefully

and sensitively.

- Recognize the energy put into the mediation, the conciliatory gestures, and any movement that may have been visible at any time.

- Check what the parties plan to do if the dispute resurfaces, if some issues are unresolved (for example how they plan to continue negotiating, or who else they might involve).
- Encourage them to take the most constructive route forward.
- Help them establish some groundrules or guidelines for future communication if they wish, or if they really seem to need them.
- Get feedback on how they have experienced the mediation process.
- Be as positive as possible about the outcome, affirm the parties' efforts, and thank them for their participation.

Mediating managers should also ensure that they have time very soon after a mediation session to talk through any difficult moments or issues, get feedback on their skills, and close on any administrative tasks. This is easier when you have colleagues in similar roles using this approach, as you can set up some kind of peer support system.

8
Mediating a High-Conflict Situation

This chapter explains how to use mediation skills and the mediation process to move forward in a complex dispute, involving allegations of sexism, bullying, and high levels of feeling. We concentrate on working with the parties in a joint session.

CASE STUDY
OZONE

Setting

Selina Buckingham (a graduate in her early 30s, three years in the company) reports to Bruce Lord (a graduate in his early 50s, eleven years in the company). They work for a world-leading pharmaceutical company that is in its third year after a merger.

It was universally agreed that the merger was financially sensible, but that the two organizations had some significant clashes of culture. OZO was perceived to be traditional, hierarchical, and generally safe in its management and HR philosophies. Onechem saw itself as an innovator in production, promotion, and management and HR practices. It had recently introduced competency-based recruitment and performance management systems, which were now being implemented over the whole new organization, OZONE.

Selina came from Onechem and Bruce from OZO. Over the last two years resentment has been building and a number of people in their team and outside have expressed concerns that a really damaging conflict is brewing, one that cannot afford to be seen as a test of strength or a battle between the two old wings of the company.

Kola Fajimola, the regional research manager responsible for the team in which Selina and Bruce work, has witnessed the growing feud. Recently a public argument at a team meeting led to each of them independently asking for a meeting with him. He scheduled these meetings with mediation in mind.

What Kola was told initially by Selina is that she feels Bruce is a draconian manager, who has overstepped the mark into bullying her. She wants something done about it and intends to take out a grievance under the new "fair treatment" policy. Kola manages to persuade her to hold off, as he might be able to help by holding a private, problem-solving meeting. Selina is skeptical, but is prepared to wait until she has sat down with Kola since she feels she has nothing to lose.

Bruce phones Kola the same day, confirming that he too is upset and embarrassed that the acrimony between the two has been spilling over into the office for three or four months. There have been a number of angry exchanges. Bruce thinks that Selina is "out to get him" by starting a grievance; he realizes that this could look very bad for him, but is furious about what he feels are unjust claims. He, too, is willing to put a couple of hours aside with Kola to sort it out. If not, "he'll be out of OZONE like a shot."

RIPENESS FOR MEDIATION

This may look like a high-pressure, high-risk situation, but it has some ingredients that make it ideal for a mediation-style approach. Kola knows that his mediation skills will be tested to the full, but is prepared to go ahead with a joint session because:

■ Both people agree to try it.
■ Both parties have issues that they urgently want to settle.
■ The issues are within the parties' control.
■ There is a need for immediate action.
■ The power balance is potentially able to be bridged.
■ Neither party really wants a formal investigation.
■ Both parties recognize the value of appearing reasonable.

■ The consequences of not trying mediation could be serious.
■ Avoidance is not an option, as the pressure of work and change is great; this is a small team and the two people's work paths cross every day.

The core mediation skills outlined in this chapter are:

■ Sorting the issues into what can and can't be taken forward.
■ Managing anger and aggression.
■ Advanced facilitation.

CORE SKILL 1: SORTING THE ISSUES INTO WHAT CAN AND CAN'T BE TAKEN FORWARD

THE CONCEPT

In high-conflict cases the material located in the conflict zone is often complex and includes several ingredients. Selina and Bruce could potentially clash on various items in their conflict zone, described in Figure 6.

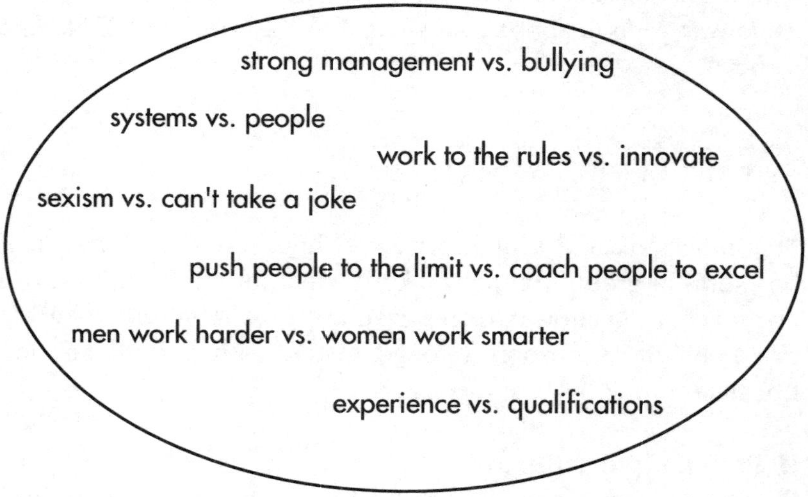

strong management vs. bullying

systems vs. people

work to the rules vs. innovate

sexism vs. can't take a joke

push people to the limit vs. coach people to excel

men work harder vs. women work smarter

experience vs. qualifications

Figure 6 Selina and Bruce's conflict zone

Kola is planning to help focus Selina and Bruce on the things on which they can realistically move forward. Although it helps, people do not need to have identical values and beliefs in order to cooperate. In mediation at work some common ground usually does emerge even when people's views are diametrically opposed, as they seem to be here.

If you really want to give yourself and the parties the maximum chance of resolving a dispute, help them focus on:

- Specific complaints about behavior, money, or objects.
- Issues that the parties have the power to settle.
- Issues on which both parties are prepared to work.
- Issues that both parties have sufficient power to negotiate on and resolve.
- Issues that affect the future relationship of the parties.

Although a mediating manager can help facilitate a discussion on the following, it would not be appropriate to use mediation to resolve situations involving:

- Issues that require decisions by a higher authority (although in some cases mediated agreements can be mapped out and then ratified by law).
- Issues of basic human rights.
- Issues that require expert knowledge or technical verification.

As the purposes of mediation include clarifying misunderstandings, recognizing differences, and becoming more empathetic, there may often be non-specific issues that need to be discussed and explored, but that cannot be mediated to an agreement. Mediation is not the forum for deciding whose values are right, but it can be very productive for parties to talk about values and beliefs to each other, to build understanding.

People may want validation of their opinions and feelings about the other party or the situation, e.g., "Andy has no right to be angry." Those feelings and opinions can be heard, but no one will receive validation, or contradiction, from a mediating manager.

While discussing values is enlightening, in mediation you want to draw the parties away from discussions of values into conversations about what they want from one another. Interpretations of reality are often exchanged during joint sessions, e.g., "His problem is he thinks he owns the place." "She just can't take a joke." People make guesses about others' motives, e.g., "They're doing it on purpose." Kola is aware that Selina and Bruce may want to keep the arena of the conflict as wide as possible. In this way they can be sure of continuing to feel badly about each other.

**KEY LEARNING POINT
REDUCING THE CONFLICT ZONE**

Mediating managers seek to limit the focus in complex, high-conflict cases, without seeming not to listen or be restrictive. The parties may have values and beliefs that clash profoundly, but this does not rule out the possibility of practical agreements or mutual understanding and recognition. Keep the focus on behavior and practical matters, hear feelings and perceptions, but under no circumstances attempt to resolve whose perceptions and beliefs are right.

THE SKILL

To help parties identify issues suitable for mediation:

- Ask open questions to explore all the issues.
- When issues arise that appear difficult to mediate, ask more specific or challenging questions to clarify how important they are to the parties.
- Emphasize that all issues can be raised, but assess the likelihood of getting an agreement or having open discussion.
- Reframe abstract issues as behavioral ones. For example, "Selina, you say that respect is important to you. Can you describe some specific things that people do to let you know they respect you?"
- Explore all issues fully enough to identify key concerns and agree some sort of priority.
- Reflect the fact that you are identifying what can be resolved for the future—solutions—and not deciding who was right or wrong, reasonable or not—the past. Ask the parties what they would like to do, for example "You will probably never know how, or why, the papers went astray. What would you like to do to make sure that it does not happen again?"

■ Reflect all the issues in outline, identifying which are the most appropriate for discussion and why.

KEY LEARNING POINT
TAKING TIME TO EXPLORE

Remember that mediating managers are there to help parties work out a way forward on their issues. The main concerns may not be immediately identifiable and the conflict could comprise non-specific issues relating to values and beliefs. The opposite is also possible, with the parties wanting to bring in every issue they can think of, e.g., in this case the merger, the logo, the role of women and men in society, the value of qualifications, etc. Mediating managers work with the parties in the separate sessions to enable them to feel comfortable enough to disclose what their issues are, but not to bring everything from their conflict zone into the room.

Keeping a positive focus, reminding parties what they are there for and what can be achieved, will help the parties retain rapport with you while they are deciding what to discuss and what not to bring to the table. At joint meetings the best place in the process to agree an agenda is after uninterrupted time and the initial exploration of issues in stage 5.

When Kola asks Selina to outline her issues in the joint session she is fuming: "He's been making my life an absolute misery."

Kola listens without interrupting and manages any interruptions from Bruce. Kola starts to jot down a few notes to help him remember and to prompt him to ask follow-up questions. Selina notices, but does not slow down. Eventually she pauses and Kola explains the notes. He then uses them to summarize back to her what she has said.

When it is Bruce's turn he starts by saying, "She may have passed her MBA, but she knows nothing about staff, and even less about detailed research." He continues in this vein, outlining in very general terms for a few minutes what he thinks of Selina and criticizing her for what she cannot do.

In order to be fair, Kola acknowledges Bruce's frustration and seeks to move him from blaming comments to practical issues: "I can see how having a member of staff who you do not think is, in your words, 'up for the task' is difficult. Could you perhaps give me a couple of examples of this, what you have done to manage it, and what the result has been?"

Little by little Bruce's issues emerge. He believes that he has to manage Selina firmly, as she is not pulling her weight in the department. No one else in the team finds his "firm and down-to-earth management style" difficult. He has no problems with women, and believes that Selina often offers herself for jobs beyond her capability because she is "good in theory," but "not so good in real life." Bruce also thinks that Selina is careless, for example for having left her laptop, with lots of company details in it, on the back seat of her car. It was stolen, but quickly recovered intact by police.

Kola reflects these issues back, checks for more, and pauses. He now helps Bruce and Selina explore and sort their issues. There are six key issues according to Selina. Bruce constantly criticizes her work on minor points; sets unrealistic workloads; makes inappropriate personal comments, often of a sexist nature; is patronizing and treats her like a child or an undergraduate who has no practical experience; "he is really creepy and doesn't seem to have any friends and he should never have been made manager in the new set-up."

Kola explores the first four points, gets examples, and probes for more information. Selina looks calmer. When asked, she says that she feels better. Kola now does some work to identify what Selina wants and to encourage her out of her conflict zone.

He explains that she is entitled to her opinions of Bruce, but he wants to clarify which of the issues Selina wants to bring to Bruce's attention. They agree that the first four will form the focus, and Kola goes on to explain how he would like to take this forward and how the joint meeting will work, and repeats the groundrules using a very targeted phrase: "When we get to the time to move forward, I will ask you both to concentrate on the practical issues that are within your domain."

Bruce launches into another tirade against Selina. He brings in issues about her style of dress and personal life. Kola interrupts and steers Bruce away from the personal material: "Bruce, you feel strongly about the way that Selina lives her life. When *you concentrate only on that I feel disappointed, because the practical managerial issues are the ones I believe you want to address. I would like it if you could concentrate on these now."*

CORE SKILL 2: MANAGING ANGER AND AGGRESSION

When we feel angry we often experience tunnel vision: We exclude views and information that are outside the tunnel, and we see only one destination or outcome. The feeling of anger, and the response it frequently gets, fuel our behavior. Behaviors may then become fixed in particular patterns, which are not necessarily constructive for us or the other people involved. Our capacity to show empathy for others often goes down, as does our ability to problem solve. Instead we tend to fight about the problem and the solution. Communication is also affected and we may listen less, hearing only what we want or expect to hear. As emotion increases we may not be so interested in the truth, instead being fixed on maintaining our own position and "winning."

The feeling of anger is always valid. It is a signal that something is wrong between us and the outside world, or within our needs and beliefs. We may judge ourselves and others harshly when anger is present, but it is more useful to experience the anger, identify its source, and work on achieving whatever changes are necessary to rectify what is wrong.

Anger can materialize in different ways. Angry behavior may be:

- An appropriate expression of feeling.
- A displaced expression or feeling (aimed at a person but not directly to do with them, or about a particular event but not really caused by it).
- A confused expression of feeling (when people feel fear they often express anger).
- A ritual or tantrum behavior with the goal of getting attention, control, communicating helplessness, or gaining revenge.
- A purposeful behavior with the goal of intimidating or confusing the "target."

THE CONCEPT

The iceberg of aggression

Other people's aggression is powerful and may well disturb us. We need to recognize that aggressive behavior is a sign that something is not right for the person concerned, that needs are not being met. A number of feelings could trigger aggressive behavior but, as with an iceberg, we see only the tip. It is difficult to determine what is underneath. Aggressive behavior may be caused by hurt, embarrassment, frustration, fear, confusion, or pain.

Managing ourselves when anger and aggression are present

When other people are angry or aggressive toward us, or toward others in our vicinity, a whole set of habits, assumptions, and reactions can be triggered off.

For many years on our training programs we have run an exercise in which we dramatize a bus queue where an unexpected argument happens between two people. Everyone else is asked to react as if it is real. Some people want to run away, others take sides, others intervene assertively. Many people become aware of signs of arousal in their body: changes in temperature and breathing, or sickness in the pit of their stomach.

It is important to recognise what our threshold of anxiety is around other people's anger. These signals in our body are like early-warning systems, telling us that there may be a moment of threat.

You should not have to stretch your own level of safety and comfort too much in mediation-style sessions. There are a number of factors about your role as a mediating manager that should help you cope skillfully with other people who become angry or aggressive:

■ You are an onlooker to the anger or aggression, not a target of it.
■ The anger or aggression is not there because of you.
■ You have been given permission by the parties to interrupt as appropriate.
■ Few, if any, of your values or needs are at stake.

**KEY LEARNING POINT
MANAGING ANGER AND AGGRESSION**

Anger and aggression should not be excluded from disputes, but should rather be acknowledged, responded to non-defensively, and channeled. A mediating manager will offer nothing that might hook into the unmet needs that are causing people to be angry or aggressive. Because mediation is so sharply focused on needs, it often significantly reduces the aggression that has already been present in a dispute.

When angry or aggressive feelings or behavior emerge in a mediated dispute, the mediating manager will need to:

THE SKILL

- Pay attention.
- Manage their own response.
- Create a safe environment in which to sustain dialogue.
- Channel the angry feelings and behavior.
- Create an opportunity to move beyond the anger and aggression to what people need.

Once you have assessed an interruption as being necessary, there are three steps to defusing aggression constructively (see Table 13). If the behavior continues you may need to repeat the three steps, and use another, possibly more directive, control or facilitation strategy.

The traffic light approach

Table 13 The traffic light approach

Red light—Interrupt	Amber light—Pause	Green light—Move on
Use clear, non-threatening, verbal and non-verbal stop signals to get everyone's attention.	Hold everyone's attention. Check out how people are feeling about what is going on. Reflect neutrally what you are noticing. Use appropriate conflict management strategies.	Invite parties to continue with a new communication strategy in place. Watch and listen.

Selina and Bruce are nervous and determined. They arrive for their joint meeting with Kola at the same time, but avoid eye contact and sit down without saying a word. Kola thanks them for coming, introduces the session and asks Selina to speak first.

Bruce shrugs dejectedly and Selina starts, saying, "Well, thank you for giving me the chance to speak first for once, Kola."

Bruce immediately interrupts, indignantly, "Don't start. I thought this was supposed to be respectful. You just don't know the meaning of the word, do you?"

Selina responds (to Kola), "See what I said? He has the self-control of a Jack Russell terrier!"

Kola leans forward and raises his hands slightly, catching the pair's eyes. "Selina, Bruce (pause). You both have a lot to say. I know this is not easy for either of you. Bruce, you will get your chance. Selina, just concentrate on your issues."

Kola keeps interruptions to a minimum for the next 20 minutes by using the traffic light sequence two or three times. Uninterrupted time passes by tensely, but without any more direct shows of aggression.

KEY LEARNING POINT
TAKING AN INCREMENTAL APPROACH TO
AGGRESSIVE BEHAVIOR

At the early stages of a joint mediation session the mediating manager is particularly tough on aggressive behavior. As the process develops, a more relaxed approach is adopted when strong feelings are expressed, particularly if the signs are that people are comfortable and still participating fully in the session. Letting angry behavior continue is often useful, as new ideas may emerge. While you watch an argument you may also notice feelings being exchanged, listening taking place, and parties responding to rather than ignoring one another.

When to interrupt an argument

The parties are speaking rapidly, in raised voices, and conflict is present, but sometimes it can be productive. The questions in Table 14 can help you decide whether to intervene or not.

Table 14 When to interrupt an argument

Allow the argument to continue when...	Interrupt an argument when...
Parties are saying new things, exchanging new information.	Parties keep repeating themselves and going off the issues.
Parties seem equally comfortable and able to hold their own in the exchange.	Anyone seems frightened or intimidated.
Parties are hearing one another and responding to one another's statements.	Parties are seeming increasingly rigid in their positions.
	Accusations or name calling are becoming brutal or deliberately hurtful.

The most useful response to anger is an assertive one. Generally, however, anger is met with less useful passive, manipulative, or aggressive responses (see Table 15).

Assertiveness

Table 15 Assertiveness is the best response to anger

Passive Behavior based on lack of respect for yourself	Manipulative Behavior based on lack of respect for yourself and others	Aggressive Behavior based on lack of respect for others	Assertive Behavior based on respect for yourself and others
Plead for the behavior to stop.	Refuse to see or recognize the behavior, minimize it.	Give yourself permission to get angry because of their behavior.	Recognize and acknowledge their feelings.
Cry, walk out in tears.	Pretend that nothing is happening.	Blame others, using labeling language.	Accept their right to feel the way they do.
Become very quiet and unresponsive.	Deny your own feelings and gloss over theirs.	Selectively listen, waiting for a trigger.	State your own feelings clearly, unambiguously, and neutrally.
Play the martyr, take the blame on yourself.	Try to change the subject.	Refuse to move forward: "Yes, but you said earlier..."	Use neutral language and avoid blaming labels.
Give up, withdraw.	Insist on a break or a change "so we can all calm down."	Twist words, deliberately mishear.	Request a change in behavior, explaining motivationally why.
Become inarticulate and unable to express your needs, blame the person from preventing you from speaking.	Seek a third party to pacify the angry person, but in reality to "stand up" for you.	Shout back, stating your rights.	Adjust your initial position to find something you can agree on.
	Make it stop: soothe, build bridges.	Judge their right to be angry.	Stay calm.

Four-step assertiveness sequence

The DESC sequence is particularly useful when you are asking people to change their behavior:

- **Describe** what you are experiencing/noticing, using neutral, non-blaming language.
- **Explain** its effect on you.
- **Show** that you understand how others feel and the positive intention behind their behavior.
- **Communicate** your preferred alternative.

For example, if someone is looking out of the window for long periods during a joint session:

- **Describe**—Manjit, I notice you're looking out of the window.
- **Explain**—I feel concerned that you may be missing out on the benefits of this session by not taking part.
- **Show understanding**—I understand it may be difficult for you to listen to some of the things being said.
- **Communicate an alternative**—Could you just reassure me that you are still listening and happy to continue?

Or if someone is banging on the table and shouting:

- **Describe**—Bruce, when you bang on the table and shout...
- **Explain**—...I find it hard to concentrate and am missing what you are saying.
- **Show understanding**—I understand that you may be angry and frustrated and that you are trying to make your point.
- **Communicate an alternative**—I would like to hear your point, so please could you talk it through now more quietly so that I can hear what you're saying?

Neutral language

The language we use about other people contains many direct and indirect messages about our opinions, our emotions, and our concerns. When responding to angry and aggressive behavior and problem solving with other people, it is useful to use language that excludes our own views and emotions where these are unhelpful or judgmental.

Neutral language sends a message to the parties that we are not joining in, blaming, or judging. It avoids the use of judgmental phrases or words, is descriptive rather than interpretive (says what people are doing, not what they are like), and seeks to be specific rather than general. Neutral language should not reduce the importance of what is being described or significantly change the content.

The benefits to the parties of mediators using neutral language are:

■ In separate sessions it can help them to reflect on their own feelings, opinions, and concerns.

Selina: "Bruce is a complete slime ball, who has about as much idea about charm as a dead fly."
Kola: "So you are uncomfortable around Bruce? What about him as a manager?"

■ In joint sessions people may be more likely to hear and respond to the other person.

Bruce: "She's so full of herself, yet she can't produce the goods."
Kola: "You are not happy with Selina's performance, Bruce?"

■ The other person can also choose language that is less conflictual, e.g., focusing on responsibility rather than blame.

Kola: "I wonder if you could put across to Selina what she can do to help you work with her more effectively?"
Bruce: "Well she can get off her backside..."
Kola: "Hold on, Bruce. So what action do you want from Selina?"

Kola is generally perceived as calm under pressure, but after an hour of hostile exchanges he is getting tired of persistent angry and aggressive phrases and the lack of progress in the meeting. He becomes aware that Selina and Bruce are comfortable with their conflict. It has defined their relationship for as long as they can remember and they are reluctant to let it go. Kola will need to be creative in his attempts to move them forward.

Table 16 Uses of neutral language in mediation

Reflecting and summarizing to:	**Requesting changes in behavior to:**
Enable the other party to hear.	Exercise control without blaming.
Encourage self-reflection by the speaker.	Defuse aggression.
Redirect potentially destructive behavior.	Keep parties participating.
Encourage the identification of interests.	

CORE SKILL 3: ADVANCED FACILITATION

THE CONCEPT

At any stage in a dispute there may be problems with the interaction between the parties: There may be limited movement on the content and the process might seem stuck. Mediators are ready for this and have a bank of techniques to address these problems and move people on.

THE SKILLS

Moving the interaction on

■ **Working on what is going on in the room**—sometimes the behavior in the room is absolutely typical of what happens when two people get together in negative conflict. The mediator can help by reflecting this back to the parties to check whether they have noticed that they are slipping into familiar territory; and encourage them to try a different style of interaction.

Kola: "Bruce and Selina, I don't know if you have noticed. You make an offer, Bruce, usually adding 'love' or 'dear,' and Selina, you say 'I'm not your dear' and do not respond to, or appear to hear, the offer. How about missing out 'dear,' Bruce, and Selina, how will you respond this time?"

■ **Setting boundaries and shepherding**—keep the discussion within agreed or useful guidelines, for example only discussing one issue at a time. Encourage and nurture the parties, for example by emphasizing the positives, reminding them why they are there.
■ **Getting people to say what they want**—rather than what they think of one another.

Kola: "Bruce, you've said Selina is 'wet behind the ears.' Selina, you described Bruce as a 'draconian' manager. You then went into a long exchange about the past. What do you want from Bruce as a manager, Selina, and what do you want from Selina as a team member, Bruce?"

- **Emphasizing conciliatory gestures**—e.g., "She said that she did not really give you a chance, and things would be different if..."
- **Showing understanding of mutual feelings**—e.g., "I can see that you were both really upset about that."
- **Keeping silent and letting the parties get on with it**—as mediation progresses the parties may well feel much more willing and able to challenge one another, to express their feelings, and to respond directly to one another. The more this can be encouraged the better, provided that people seem safe and things appear to be moving.
- **Moving from the blame frame to the aim frame**—e.g., "I know that you still feel very angry about what happened. What would you hope to achieve today? How would you like things to be different next time you have a meeting?"
- **Reflecting on the give and take or fairness score**—get a sense of how close people are to achieving their goals.

Kola: "We seem to have agreed that project allocation should not happen at staff meetings, but I am not sure how you feel about progress generally. How do you think it is going so far? What can we do to move things forward?"

- **Transmitting information**.

Moving the content on

Kola: "So Selina is willing to work later on Thursdays, Bruce. I am not sure you registered that. What do you think?"

- **Checking communication**.

Kola: "Selina, did you hear what Bruce said?" or "Selina and Bruce, what are the issues on the table so far?"

■ **Recycling information**.

Kola: "What about that suggestion made earlier, about the timing of the group meeting? Bruce said that setting up the room could be shared by two volunteers."

■ **Being the agent of reality**—give clear, tactful information about what is possible and what is not.

Kola: "Whole team meetings are not possible every week, you both said that before" or "We cannot resolve that here as you do not have authority to make that decision."

■ **Parking and banking issues**—leave aside difficult issues for the moment, really register the value of successes, and recycle them if necessary.
■ **Concreteness**—break topics into bite-sized chunks. Translate general remarks into specifics, so that "He's a pain" becomes "He phones me twice a day" or "You need to be more considerate" becomes "I need my bin to be for my own use only." Keep people focused on the subject or issue at hand.

Moving the process on

■ **Controlling and signposting the process**—ensure that everyone gets a chance to contribute and regulate turn taking. Structure the discussion, e.g., keep going with suggestions rather than making decisions. Let people know how they are doing and where they are heading.
■ **Equality routines**—make sure that you do not always start with one party. Ask everyone to answer general questions, such as "What can you offer?" or "What do you think of that?" Ensure that everyone is asked for their perspective on the process.
■ **Time-outs**—take a silent break within the session, or request a 5–10-minute break.

Kola: "I think I would like a break to think about where we are going next. Perhaps you could both think about what you need to break this deadlock during the break?"

■ **Side meetings**—sometimes requesting separate meetings with both parties will allow you to check things out that might be difficult in joint sessions, and side meetings also often allow the parties to think more clearly, particularly if the joint session has been loud and difficult.

Kola calls a break after an hour and uses the quiet space to jot down what he believes has been achieved so far and the status of unresolved issues. Selina and Bruce are not getting past their personal hostility and are threatening to revert to formal action to sort this out. When the session reconvenes, Kola summarizes where he believes they have reached so far.

"First, thanks for coming back. I am glad you are prepared to put more time aside. I think you realize that if this is not resolved today, you will have missed a great opportunity. You've agreed to differ about management styles, but Selina has acknowledged that she does not work as hard on projects led by you as she does ones led by herself. Bruce, you asked for weekly one-to-ones, but in the end we agreed every other week. Selina requested that you do not call her 'dear' or 'love,' and although you say you meant nothing by it, you agree. I think it is now time to go beyond the qualifications versus experience argument, and focus on the manager–team member relationship. Don't forget, you both agreed that a move to another job was not possible. So, how are you going to redefine the groundrules between you?"

Bruce: "I don't want Selina to be so difficult when I'm trying to be pleasant!"

Kola: "What do you want, Bruce?"

Bruce: "I want weekly timesheets for the next two months so that I can keep better track of Selina."

Selina: "I'm not bothered about the timesheets. As long as he doesn't patronize me at staff meetings."

Bruce goes to react. Kola: "Hold on, Bruce. Let me just check what Selina means by that."

Selina: "I mean, look me in the face, talk to me like the other team members. Manage me firmly by all means, but don't treat me like I'm two years old. I don't need memos and emails saying the same thing."

Bruce: "But you sometimes don't look at emails."

Selina: "I always do. There was just that one."

Kola sits back and lets them go on, as they are, at long last, having a conversation. Their body language is less confrontational and their tone is more adult. Every time they pause he captures what they have discussed and agreed. After a total of 90 minutes they emerge, still disliking one another, but with a clear structure and set of groundrules for future working between them.

9

Using Mediation for Group Disputes

Groups have been part of working life for as long as there has been work. They serve a practical and social function. People come together in groups to pursue and achieve higher goals, targets, and output than they could otherwise individually manage. A variety of relationships and roles is also available in workgroups to help us develop our sense of self in relation to others, and to allow us the exercise of our social, interactive skills.

Consequently, when negative conflict develops in groups it damages functioning and output, and often causes substantial harm to an individual's sense of self-worth as well as to relationships within the group.

This chapter illustrates how a mediation-style approach can quickly rebuild teams that are breaking up over conflict, and also looks at mediation as a tool for the effective resolution of difficult and complex inter-group disputes, for example those about pay and conditions. This approach is most effective when responsibility for difficulties is shared; power imbalances and hierarchies are manageable; and people are prepared to concentrate on common goals and work constructively through competitive or conflicting goals. It will not be as effective if there is a clear case of a victim and perpetrator; if a higher-level adjudication is required; or if people are unable or unwilling to work through their differences.

CASE STUDY
A TEAM ON THE POINT OF COLLAPSE

Setting

Action Assist is part of a major national social housing provider in the UK, specializing in care services for the elderly. This business unit has been set up to provide in-home care for elderly people within the community, including physical and medical care, financial advice, and support with general welfare issues. The local office employs four full-time staff and three part-time, all of whom deliver care to clients in their homes. The director of operations, Winifred Li, is responsible for securing resources, managing contracts, and developing the organization, and spends a great deal of time out of the office, liaising with other agencies, clients' families, and local authorities who buy in services from Action Assist. Agnes, the unit manager, is responsible for the day-to-day running of the organization and supervising the staff who deliver the care.

Winifred and Agnes stopped communicating several months ago. At staff meetings Winifred barely looks at Agnes, and Agnes treats Winifred as though she is invisible. They work together when necessary, but mechanically and without real communication or consultation, on issues of mutual concern. Winifred works strictly to her role, focusing on contract negotiation and maintenance, client liaison and strategic issues. Agnes gets on with day-to-day work and supervision. If a client wants to speak about a contract issue they speak to Winifred, and a staffing or care issue is directed to Agnes.

This compartmentalization is making the organization function clumsily, duplicate work, and work reactively. Staff are unsure who to go to if they have a joint issue involving contracts and day-to-day care. Some clients have also experienced difficulties in raising long-term issues to do with their care, for example what is covered and what is not, because it is often difficult to get contract information from Winifred. She has her own filing system and non-networked computer.

Head office has noticed the tension, which is "tangible" when regional manager Olivia visits the office. Staff have spoken to her about an incident nine months ago that may have sparked this off, involving a disclosure that Agnes made about Winifred in a staff meeting. No one is keen to say much more than that. Olivia also believes that there may be cultural issues, since Winifred's cultural heritage is a mixture of Chinese and English and Agnes is Scottish. Winifred has also spoken in confidence with Olivia about her colleague's "racism," but as yet has chosen not to make that concern public with a formal grievance.

The day-to-day running of the organization has become stressed and difficult. Staff members have different allegiances and divisions are beginning to appear. Very recently a staff member who has worked very closely for many years with Agnes refused to attend a visit to a potential new client with Winifred, because "she had not been given sufficient notice by Winifred," who then threatened to suspend her. Procedures require consultation with a head office manager before suspending staff, and when Olivia heard of this she suggested an amnesty, while she set up a process to "get to the bottom of the situation and sort things out." Olivia is also shocked when she looks at the statistics for the last six months, which reveal a 15 percent loss of existing custom and 30 percent fall-off in new business. This is during a period that usually sees high demand.

The key ingredients of the approach outlined here are:

- Neutral assessment of the situation.
- Building a safe, collaborative environment.
- Facilitating a collaborative process of resolution.

NEUTRAL ASSESSMENT

It is almost impossible in these difficult, hurtful group conflicts for an insider truly to understand what is going on. One of the negative effects of group conflict is that people often lose their sense of what is good for the group, and revert to perceptions and behaviors that satisfy their own needs. Mutual trust is replaced by suspicion, defensiveness, and low rapport. When people request outside intervention, they do so on their own terms and generally in pursuit of their own agenda.

KEY LEARNING POINT

If you are asked to facilitate a group dispute, avoid the pitfall of basing your approach entirely on one account of events. The first stage of any group mediation is neutral assessment, which allows a comprehensive review of the issues, feelings, and concerns from all perspectives.

What needs to be explored and assessed?

Action Assist staff perceive Olivia as someone who has the skills and demeanor to help. She has their respect, but first she needs to establish that she is not too close to the situation to use a mediation-style approach. In a brief letter to everyone in the team she maps out the process, her role, and her prior knowledge of the situation. This letter abides by all the principles of mediation in that it is neutral, positive, lucid, and disciplined.

"I have suggested to Agnes and Winifred that I help you work on some of the difficult circumstances and issues that have affected your work and working relationship. I know very little about the background, other than that Agnes and Winifred admit that they have not been getting on.

My interest is in moving forward, and with your help I am sure that we can return Action Assist to being the vibrant, positive organization it was before.

I intend to meet with each of you in confidence, separately at first, so that you can tell me what's been going on from your perspective, highlight your concerns, and reflect on ways forward. I hope we can then get everyone together to discuss issues and seek ways forward.

I will tell you much more about this process when we meet, but leave you with some important key concepts. I will be impartial, looking to resolve difficulties rather than apportion blame, and helping everyone to create a constructive atmosphere for dialogue.

You will get the opportunity to clarify the issues, identify ways forward, and work together to rebuild your team. I am currently asking for your commitment to preliminary, individual meetings. I will discuss how a joint meeting would work with you all. Please let me know on [phone number and email address] if you cannot make the meeting with me at [time and date] and I will set up an alternative time."

In the separate sessions Olivia needs to discover for herself and help the parties reflect on:

- What has happened.
- What the issues are: common issues, issues specific to some individuals, issues specific to one individual.
- What people's needs are.
- Who the key stakeholders are, the people who:
  — are affected by, and can affect, the conflict.
  — have the information necessary to clarify what is happening and why.
  — have feelings that need to be heard.
  — have the authority, information, and resources to achieve change.
  — are committed to an ongoing, collaborative dispute-resolution process.

**KEY LEARNING POINT
GETTING TO THE STAKEHOLDERS**

It is not always evident at the start who the key stakeholders are or what the issues are. Outside mediators ask their contact in the client organization who they should listen to and what has been happening. Nevertheless, they frequently find that, once they are in front of the parties, they get a very different story and variations on who the significant people are. Meet with everyone you can during the assessment stage and they will help you to identify who really needs to be in the resolution stage.

Olivia plans her questions so that everyone gets a consistent approach, sequences meetings according to random selection and availability, and allows longer for Agnes and Winifred than for the others. A schedule is completed and everyone in the team is seen within two working days. There are a couple of tricky moments when Olivia's mediation skills come in very handy.

Winifred fears losing face

Winifred is very reluctant early on to engage with Olivia. She is very formal, talks generally about her work, and skirts round any probing questions. After a while Olivia checks out what is happening, working on the hunch that what is normal and OK for her in this role may not be so for Winifred.

Olivia: "You look uncomfortable as we speak, Winifred, and I want to make sure that I am not working in a way that is inappropriate for you. Could you let me know how you are feeling right now?"

Winifred: "This is not of my making. I am being dragged here at my manager's insistence, and will be paraded in front of the team. I find this insulting and unhelpful. This is not your problem, but mine."

Olivia (using the three Es; see pages 76): "You are unhappy about the mediation. Are you concerned about how public this is?"

Winifred: "This will look extremely bad for me. I am the most senior person here. I should be making decisions, but that is being taken away from me."

Olivia: "I think I understand your discomfort now. You see this process as undermining your position as director, and the negative effect it might have on your reputation and standing in the team." (Pause to check. Winifred nods to confirm.)

Olivia: "That is not the intention of the process. These separate meetings are off the record, so that people can say what they need to. It is possible to take a step-by-step approach, if people don't want to go straight to a full team meeting. Neither you nor anyone else would be asked to participate in a joint meeting unless you were clear about the benefits and willing. The whole focus of this process is to move forward through these difficult issues without damaging anyone."

Winifred: "Agnes will not be easy to restrain. She is loose of tongue and mind. Excellent at her job, but a talker. I am a listener."

Winifred is now speaking about her experience and continues to do so. Olivia gets the impression that a joint meeting between Agnes and Winifred is needed first, then a whole team meeting. When she proposes this to Winifred, the director offers relieved acceptance. So far so good.

Agnes is the final person to be seen. Everyone else apart from Winifred will meet in whatever format is suggested. Winifred prefers a separate session with Agnes first. Agnes feels as though Winifred is not "good with the team. She is aloof, doesn't delegate well, and treats me as though I am an underling some of the time. She set this up, of course, it's her baby, but it's the team who have made it into a real service. I want this to be treated as a team issue, or I'm not going to attend."

Olivia acknowledges what Agnes has said and asks what she hopes to achieve out of the session.

"I want Winifred to know that we are all in this together. She has become really closed off since that staff meeting to discuss training and development. She should explain to us all why she is so awkward now, with that filing system of hers, and things under lock and key."

Olivia explores what the issues are for Agnes, then checks whether things were always like this. She is seeking to take time out of Agnes and Winifred's conflict zone, which is loaded with crossed cultural expectations and different styles of communication. Agnes admits that they got on really well to begin with. When asked what changed, Agnes talks about the notorious staff meeting in detail. Winifred had had a conversation with her beforehand, explaining that her own computer skills were very low and that she relied on her husband to do much of the report writing because it took her so long. Agnes referred to this in the meeting so that Winifred could seem more human, more accessible to the staff. "It was meant with the best of intentions, but Winifred took it the wrong way. She went so far, after the meeting, as to say she felt betrayed. We have not really spoken a friendly word since."

Olivia cannot reveal what Winifred said, but she knows that these two need to talk about this event and move on. This, in her view, is the only way the team can make progress together.

Olivia: "What would you say to a meeting between you and Winifred, to get to the bottom of that incident? You and she are coming at it from completely different perspectives. I could organize a private room, with me there to help the dialogue, to help you bridge the gap between you. That would be better for both of you and the team. Then, of course, it will be easier to focus on the team."

Agnes is for the team not the individual

Agnes agrees, provided that the team meeting is not ruled out, and she explains that she would like to get across to Winifred that the latter's manner is not helpful.

Two days later Agnes and Winifred meet, and Agnes quickly realizes that she has wounded Winifred. She apologizes and requests some time to explain what she was seeking to do. Winifred listens, Agnes talks, and soon they recognize that the events following the meeting could have been handled more effectively. Tension is still in the air, as they both feel that the impact of their disagreement on the business has been severe and that the team may harbor feelings about that. The team meeting will have to be handled delicately, to avoid opening old wounds and causing new ones.

KEY LEARNING POINT

Not all group dispute-resolution processes are run with the whole group present. Sometimes, as in this case, some specific small group work is necessary to deal with conflicts and issues that are specific to only some of the individuals, or matters that would affect the chances of resolution if they were not managed separately first.

BUILDING A SAFE, COLLABORATIVE ENVIRONMENT

The individual sessions allow an independent facilitator, using a mediation-style approach, to start working on the relationship between the parties, as well as the practical aspects of the dispute. "A good working relationship provides the collaborative spirit necessary to create the imaginative and resourceful options needed to satisfy many parties' interests. When both sides are looking at scarce resources and a dissatisfied community as a shared problem, rather than focusing their energy on attacking each other, they generate better options."[1]

In the separate sessions, during the assessment stage, Olivia is working conscientiously to build up a sense that the way for-

ward will be safe, and that a collaborative process is possible. She is modeling collaborative working by using reflective listening, exploring needs and acknowledging feelings, and encouraging people to see her as a facilitator, not a judge. Olivia also gets each of the parties to think seriously about how best to work through their differences and concentrate on common goals. She invites their participation in designing the process, which builds their confidence that their needs will be met. Once they have described their situation and what they think has happened, everyone is asked the following questions:

- ■ "Which of the issues you have raised do you think would best be brought to the joint meeting? How could the issue be framed in such a way as not to minimize it, but also not to personalize it?"
- ■ "What do you think might stop you getting the most for yourself and the team out of this meeting? What can I, you, and others do to help you get the most out of this?"
- ■ "What do you want from the time and what do you contribute to it? What goals do you think you share with the team?"

KEY LEARNING POINT

Inviting people into a process and seeking their assistance in tailoring it to their needs constitute an effective rapport-building tool. This also alerts the mediating manager to some of the possible substantive and process difficulties ahead. Thinking ahead creatively about possible hurdles to resolution allows people to rehearse positive approaches to hurdles and get into the right frame of mind to work through difficult moments.

Groundrules are also clarified and signposted so that people know what is expected of them, as well as what help the facilitator can, and cannot, offer. A full day is set aside, with the broad goal of understanding the issues holding the team back and making a start on rebuilding performance and confidence.

Olivia outlines briefly, at the end of each individual session, how joint meetings with groups are structured and what the *groundrules are. Essentially, the structure is the same as in a joint mediation meeting. Olivia explains that she will be working with a support mediator who will help "capture issues, summarize discussion and assist us in making the most of the session." This person is supported and constrained by the same groundrules as everyone else. Amelia, the trainer for the region, is known to everyone and they are all willing for her to attend.*

FACILITATING A COLLABORATIVE PROCESS OF RESOLUTION

Once everyone is in the room and settled, Olivia goes through the structure and purpose of the session. Before initiating uninterrupted time, she introduces a team-building exercise.

She asks everyone to think about what this team is good at when it is at its best. Everyone is asked to contribute and she notes their suggestions on a flipchart, as a visual record of the team's capacity. There follows a day of intense activity, which tests all the mediator's skills, but eventually the conflict dissipates and the team resets its levels of rapport. In the past it did not matter that Agnes and Winifred had different approaches to people, and again everyone realizes that you do not have to be the same to work together.

Rather than giving a blow-by-blow account of the dispute, here is a checklist of useful interventions that help in moving toward a satisfactorily negotiated settlement.

CHECKLIST
USEFUL INTERVENTIONS

■ **Facilitating communication and developing cooperative patterns of interactions**—"Could you say that to Agnes?" "What would work if that will not?" "Thank you for waiting for Bill to finish."

■ **Stressing the benefits of a negotiated, as opposed to an imposed, settlement**—"You have all mentioned your desire to build the business and that head office don't understand. You're right. That's why it's better if you sort this out, not them."

■ **Helping people to overcome misunderstandings that may have accumulated in the past**—e.g., Agnes and Winifred both bring to the joint session a brief account of how they had addressed their mutual misunderstanding over the disclosure. They are guided by the mediator to stay away from what was particularly sensitive in the original situation and to reset the team's picture of this negative history.

■ **Suggesting ways of consolidating groups around shared interests if the negotiating process fragments**—sometimes different people keep making similar points and recycling the conflict, because they feel disparate and are seeking a voice. Olivia moved the process on by asking people to select an area they wanted to work on and to come up with ideas for resolution together.

■ **Looking at deadlines and introducing them to help focus minds forward**—when there are no time constraints, there are no limits. Check in advance if there are any natural moments meaning that decisions need to be made by a certain time (external factors such as customer requirements) or where pauses can be taken, e.g., lunch, going home. Always explain the reasons for deadlines, whether or not they are arrived at consensually. Olivia regularly talked the clock down so that the team knew how much time they had used and how much was left.

■ **Introducing a more distributive approach**—often in groups people focus on one issue and one way forward, e.g., there is not enough money for publicity, so how can more money be made available or raised? A more distributive approach explores what marketing needs there are, how to achieve them, the different ways in which money could be spent, and what could be achieved with no expenditure. In the past Winifred had determined contracts with clients, but she now realized that other people could help to refine and tailor them, because of their experience of implementation. Winifred looked at defining contracts and how it could be improved, and the others looked at development and keeping up to date.

- **Reflecting back on group process in the room and redesigning behavioral contracts**—the groundrules are the contracts to which parties verbally consent before a mediation session begins. Sometimes they seem rather abstract and arbitrary. In group conflicts the need for behavioral contracts often becomes all too evident when people revert to habitually negative patterns in the joint sessions, having committed themselves to other, more positive behaviors at the start of the session. They are sucked in by the group dynamic, and re-enact the drama that they have played through so many times before. This time they have an audience, with a mediating manager who will draw the parties' attention to what is happening, wind down the drama, and explore why it happens and how to prevent it. This working on what is in the room creates strong adherence to, and ownership of, groundrules. Olivia regularly drew the parties' attention to non-listening behaviors and frequently surprised people with re-cycled versions of their own negative comments.

EQUALITY ROUTINES

When acting as a mediating manager you may well fall into habits that you have developed for managing groups. These are likely to involve ways of showing attention, managing content, acknowledging contributions, and dealing with strong feelings. Spontaneous, skillful responding to what the group brings is fundamental to effective mediation-style working, and many of our habits and skills will be useful. Sometimes, however, the way we interact with groups can become unbalanced, over-focused on one side or on one party, or more or less responsive to one party than the other. These unbalanced responses are directly influenced by our assumptions and expectations of the parties.

KEY LEARNING POINT
EQUALITY AND BALANCE

In order to maintain a balance, it is useful to develop some routines to ensure that you are aiming to give everyone an equal opportunity to respond to the facilitator/mediator and to one another, and to get the most out of the dispute process. These equality routines can also help to redress imbalances of power, by infiltrating the routines that have been set up to perpetuate those imbalances. For example, "I listen, you speak; I start, you follow; I propose, you support or oppose."

There are three areas in which mediating managers can develop and sustain equality routines:

Getting feedback from the parties about their experience of the process:

FEEDBACK

Avoid

✗ Avoid asking only one side if they have any questions after your opening statement.
✗ Avoid asking general questions to check how people are doing and accepting answers from some but not all parties.
✗ Avoid asking the same person first every time for feedback.

Equality routine

✔ Ask each party by name whether they have any questions of their own.
✔ Ask everyone by name how they feel the process is going, changing the sequence of who speaks first each time you get feedback.
✔ Acknowledge every response.

Asking option-generating questions to the parties:

OPTION GENERATION

Avoid

✗ Avoid giving the same person the lead role, e.g., frequently asking a question of one party and then only asking the others to respond, or always starting questions with the same person.
✗ Avoid thanking some people for their contributions and not others.

✗ Avoid not going to someone who is being "difficult" for fear of the option they may come up with.

Equality routine

✔ Ask the same question of all parties by name, reflect each answer, then encourage discussion or responses. Three sample questions: "Bill, what do you think could happen to improve the situation?" (then ask the same question of the other party); "Samir, what for you is the most important issue?"(then ask the same question of the other party); "Siobhan, what are your views on what Charity has just said?"(then ask the same question of the other party).
✔ Acknowledge all suggestions.

EMPATHY

Acknowledging feelings and showing empathy:

Avoid

✗ Avoid selective empathy or acknowledgment.
✗ Avoid unbalanced body language or tone of voice.
✗ Avoid uneven reflection of facts and feelings.

Equality routine

✔ Genuinely try to understand and show understanding of everyone's feelings, however far they may be from your own under those circumstances.
✔ Regularly check your own body language, tone, and non-verbal empathy, and understanding of all parties.
✔ Ensure that your summaries are full of information and acknowledge the feelings of all parties.

TIPS FOR INTER-GROUP DISPUTES

We round off this chapter with some ideas from the mediation toolkit that can create better processes for settling complex disputes between various groups on issues such as pay and conditions, strategic planning, and policy development.

BUILDING GOOD RELATIONSHIPS BETWEEN DIFFERENT GROUPS

Lum and Christie[2] emphasize the importance of building good working relationships between different groups in complex disputes, particularly when resources are scarce. They identify how mediation-style facilitators helped to create good working relationships between diverse stakeholders in the San Diego Schools Contract Negotiations in 2000. They worked on relationships among four general categories: among the leaders; among the bargainers; between bargainers and key stakeholders; and between the bargainers and facilitators.

The role of leaders is crucial in maintaining effective dialogue and sustaining momentum. Lum and Christie noted that, "Leaders can undermine collaboration by publicly attacking each other, by modeling and rewarding adversarial behavior, by lacking vision or direction, and by not focusing on the big picture. They were encouraged instead to emphasize the importance of working together, and creating more constructive working relationships, sending out consistent signals, refusing to bad mouth one another, remaining resilient, and staying in the process when things got tough."

There was a risk that the negotiation process would fail and people would revert to an acrimonious strike, if bargainers felt that their time was being wasted, or if they felt disengaged or let down. This risk was averted by a wise choice of team members: experienced, high-level decision makers, and people who were resistant to, as well as in favor of, the interest-based approach.

Working with the leaders

Working with relationships between bargainers

KEY LEARNING POINT
WORKING WITH A RANGE OF STAKEHOLDERS

Always include people who are resistant or critical, as they can represent the views of those who are going to be most difficult to convince. Including people who are skeptical also reassures those outside the dispute-resolution process that it is fair and open.

The relationships between members of this key group were also assisted by outside facilitation; the setting of a procedural contract that identified the goals of the group and the groundrules to which they would work; an agreement on how to interact; and a schedule for addressing issues.

Sometimes the people at the table work well together but their constituent groups resist, or veto, the suggestions that they are brought. As relationships at the table improve, some

Building credibility between bargainers and key stakeholders

hardened bargainers may also become suspicious of the process. Workshops for people who may be resistant can help build confidence. It is also important to minimize surprises, to agree to keep conflicts in the room, and to engage key skeptics in the process.

Creating focus and flexibility between facilitators and parties at the table

A loss of control, excess control, or disruptive negotiators may destroy the dispute-resolution process. This can be avoided by using multiple facilitators who can work in different ways, model positive co-working, and use their combined creativity to tackle any difficult circumstances. Initially, facilitators will be concentrating on managing the process and maintaining positive interactions and collaborative behaviors. As the participants learn appropriate values and behaviors, the facilitators take more of a back seat.

SETTING UP A STAKEHOLDER DIALOGUE

The process of stakeholder dialogue, which is used primarily in large-scale development, environmental, and public policy issues, provides some useful ideas for inter-group dispute resolution and collective bargaining. Andrew Acland offers some key pointers.[3]

1 Create an inclusive process, involving all interest groups that have a concern in the outcome. Include those who may otherwise be excluded or marginalized.
2 Use independent facilitators, applying a mediation-style approach.
3 Facilitators may or may not also be knowledgeable in the subject matter of the process. While some substantive knowledge of subjects under discussion is useful for facilitators, process skills and understanding are essential.
4 Share responsibility for the agenda and the process among all stakeholders.
5 Ensure two-way communication. Avoid public relations stunts, presentations, and formal set-piece inputs.
6 Be prepared to look at situations and issues from different perspectives, several times over, in order to seek mutually acceptable solutions.
7 People attend as equals. While different stakeholders have different responsibilities in relation to the issues under dis-

cussion, within a dialogue process stakeholders participate as equals.

8   Dialogue processes seek to identify, and build on, common ground while not denying disagreement.

9   Stakeholder dialogue tries to turn blame for the past into hope for the future through openness and a spirit of mutual learning.

10 Stakeholder dialogue processes are recorded visibly and transparently, with stakeholders having control over the content and accuracy of the recording.

REFERENCES

1   Grande Lum and Monica Christie (2001) *Adversaries to Allies: Lessons from the San Diego City Schools Contract Negotiations*, Thoughtbridge, MA, www.mediate.com.

2   ibid.

3   Acland, A (2001) *Principles and Characteristics of Stakeholder Dialogue Processes: Dialogue by Design*, Wotton-under-Edge, UK.

Part III
Day-to-Day Mediation Skills

Mediation skills are invaluable to managers on a day-to-day basis. They will help you cope with difficult situations that you know are coming, and also those that may instantly explode around you.

Chapters 10 and 11 contain:

■ One situation where you know in advance that there is a high potential for conflict.
■ One situation that happens without warning and needs instant handling.
■ Step-by-step guidance on how to manage the conflict and move the situation forward.
■ Summaries of key skills.

Chapter 12 shows how mediation skills can be particularly useful when managers are asked to investigate sensitive issues. Finally, Chapter 13 outlines how to build mediation into your organization's normal working practices.

10
Maintaining Dialogue under Pressure

Dialogue is defined by Nancy Dixon as "a special kind of talk—that affirms the person-to-person relationship between discussants and which acknowledges their collective right and intellectual capacity to make sense of the world."[1] It is not about agreement, nor is it lacking in emotion and passion. Dialogue is often difficult to achieve in the conflict zone, the place where people's beliefs, values, and behaviors clash. When you can achieve it, however, people often move forward together, build understanding, and put disagreement behind them.

CASE STUDY
CREATING A PERFORMANCE MANAGEMENT DIALOGUE USING CONVERSATION MANAGEMENT

Setting

Skylark Wilkins is HR manager at an international telecoms company. She has been in her post for 18 months and brought with her a performance-management system based on a range of competencies. Generally the system has worked well, producing a clear, broadly agreed method of assessing how people are managing their jobs and meeting targets, acknowledging those who are doing so, and supporting those who are not.

An HR adviser, Pavel Hrbaty, who has been in the company for 10 years, is line managed by Skylark and he is not so pleased with the system. After her first meeting with Pavel, Skylark believes that his overall level of performance has dropped dramatically. A recruitment drive he was organizing ran late because the adverts did not go to press on time and interviewers were double booked into interview rooms. Informal feedback from other colleagues has reached Skylark to the effect that Pavel has been slow responding to emails and generally seems to be "off line," rarely contributing much to office conversation. Skylark has also picked up something extra in her interactions with Pavel, a sense that he may have a problem with her as a black female manager. He has made a couple of comments, for example "Peter [his previous manager] didn't check up on me. He trusted me" or "I can see I am going to have to watch what I say with you."

Skylark does not want to lose Pavel, since he has a great deal of HR experience, some invaluable contacts, and a reputation as a "safe pair of hands." He was highly regarded within the company until this recent slump.

This example is fraught with "trap doors" for the manager. The conflict zone between the two players has a number of potentially explosive ingredients. At the center of the dispute are differing views about performance and performance management. Add to that the fact that they may have different views about the role of women and work, about race, and about how to do business. When the conflict zone between two parties contains so many clashing ingredients they often feed one another, causing hugely polarized, inflexible conflict.

Skylark's goals are to:

Strategy

■ *Manage the conversation to focus on the areas where change is possible, i.e., those that are specific, to do with actual events and behavior or performance.*
■ *Put her own feelings about Pavel's views to one side.*
■ *Select high-rapport behaviors.*
■ *Reduce the impact of the conflict zone between them.*

To achieve this she will:

- *Take a partnership approach, combining listening with telling.*
- *Seek an understanding of what Pavel thinks has been going on.*
- *Get him to reflect on his recent performance.*
- *Give him a non-blaming view of his performance from her perspective.*
- *Explore ways forward.*
- *Achieve some measurable outcomes to the conversation.*

GETTING HERSELF OUT OF THE CONFLICT ZONE

Skylark has to get herself emotionally and psychologically prepared to manage this difficult dialogue, so that she is not bringing her conflicting values, beliefs, and habits into the conflict zone. She does three things to prevent this.

Choosing a low-conflict, high-relationship route

She could play the tough managerial card and give Pavel a lowly rated appraisal, indicating his poor performance in a number of competencies. But for the moment she does not want to make an enemy of him, as she has much that she wants to achieve and knows that there will be controversy ahead. So she decides to use her mediation skills to achieve a desirable result and maintain a good working relationship with Pavel into the bargain. If this does not work she will take a more formal, disciplinarian approach.

Stopping her own red flags waving

"Red flags" are the things that other people do or say that get to us, hooking into some of our strongly held beliefs, fears, or basic insecurities.[2] Skylark is a skillful woman, but she knows that she can sometimes crumple in front of attractive, technically competent men. She is determined to stay focused and not let this affect her.

Taking charge of the process

Skylark decides that she will meet Pavel privately, at a neutral venue, for an off-the-record discussion (not formally part of the performance-management process), although agreed action points will be noted at its conclusion. She will set the scene, get Pavel's version of his recent performance, and then give him her feedback. They will then highlight the areas of agreement and disagreement and work on the latter, in the hope of agreeing mutually acceptable ways forward.

SETTING THE SCENE AND BUILDING RAPPORT

Skylark drops in on Pavel and asks him when he will have a moment to chat with her. He asks, "What about?"

Skylark comes right to the point, "I would like to discuss some recent performance issues and offer some support, off the record." She has used neutral language in an assertive tone and it is difficult for Pavel to say no. They set up a time that same afternoon, in a meeting room booked for the occasion.

Pavel looks anxious when he arrives, and Skylark welcomes him: "Thanks for coming. I am sure that you would like to know what this is about." She pauses, Pavel nods and says, "Well, I expect you'll tell me soon enough." Skylark frowns a little, but seeks to set Pavel at ease, by using empathy, and introducing the purpose of the meeting: "I can understand that you've got work to do, and that you probably do not want to be here, but I think that we can both benefit from meeting today. I sense that you think I'm always on your back, but I just want to get you, my most highly regarded HR adviser, back to the high standard of work you were producing six months ago."

Pavel remains quiet. Skylark briefly explains the process toward which she is working and reassures Pavel that she is seeking a way forward that will benefit them both.

He is still defensive: "So is this about the service department recruitment? Do we have to go over that again?"

"Only in outline so that we can learn from it." Skylark is in relentlessly constructive mode but rapport is still low. Time to map out the boundaries. "Basically, Pavel, I want to spend half an hour and first understand what has been going on for you at work, then give you some feedback, compare our perceptions, and identify ways forward. I am not making formal notes, but I would like to jot down some action points at the end. Do you understand? Any questions?"

REFLECTIVE LISTENING

Skylark invites Pavel to speak freely about his recent experience of working, how he thinks he has been doing, and why, starting with an open question. "So, how has work been for you recently?"

Pavel starts explaining how he feels and Skylark is fairly certain that he is dropping in some rather thinly disguised comments about her. "Things are just not the same around here any more. There's not as much camaraderie since Peter left. It's all systems, not people, now."

It would be very easy for Skylark to probe and challenge these comments, but she wants Pavel to be ready to listen to her, so she *keeps listening to him for the moment, reflecting back and moving from feelings to practicalities. "So things have changed, the spirit, some of the ways of working. How has that affected you?"*

He pauses, thinking that she is trying to catch him out. "Well, I'm still doing my job to the best of my ability, if that's what you mean."

Pavel is walking a very thin line here between dialogue and argument. Skylark knows that she could argue back or exercise her authority and cut him off. Pavel almost certainly knows on some level that he could draw Skylark into conflict. If he does he thinks he can win, as many people who start conflicts do. Skylark does not want to give him any conflict fuel back, so she continues to listen reflectively. "Talk to me about your job. What have you been pleased about, what could you have done better?"

Five minutes later Pavel has outlined some recent projects that he did well, and briefly mentioned that there had been problems with the service department recruitment, but they were not of his making. He knew that "there were some people around who blamed him. The newspapers were at fault," he claimed.

Skylark summarizes and checks that she has been accurate. He agrees that she has heard and seems to have understood.

NEUTRAL LANGUAGE

Now that Skylark has heard what Pavel had to tell her, he needs to hear what she has to tell him. She will use neutral language that is constructive and non-blaming, and avoid using generalizations.

"Now I would like to give you some feedback about what I have noticed. I will take one issue at a time, and then check that you have heard and understood. You are experienced and capable of excellent work, I am sure of that. You yourself mention that things have changed and that's uncomfortable. I think you have also hinted that I am very different from your previous manager. Under those circumstances I am pleased that you have continued to manage some projects well. The service department recruitment did seem to go wrong on a number of levels, though. Let's establish what did go wrong, then look at why, and what we can learn from that."

A little later two main areas of concern for Skylark were fed back to Pavel: an inadequate checking system that did not pick up the failure of copy to arrive at the newspapers; and not preparing ahead for potential difficulties. There was always pressure for interview and meeting space, for example. Each individual booking required an email or fax confirmation. If this did not arrive the booking was lost. Pavel knew this, but was off sick for three days and forgot to delegate the task. His bookings for interview rooms were all canceled.

This is difficult feedback for Pavel to take. Often when people find themselves in a potentially defensive situation they dig their heels in, creating a conflict zone of several interlocking beliefs and feelings. Pavel's sense of self is threatened by the notion of a woman who is more successful and more senior than he is. He knows he has performed ineffectively, but he has been unsettled by what he considers bad management. Skylark is also black, and although Pavel claims he has nothing against black people, his opinion is that Skylark "really fancies herself." This type of defensive thinking sustains many conflicts and is often met by aggressive thinking and behavior.

Skylark does not explicitly know how deep Pavel's resistance to her is, but she has picked up several levels of potential conflict. She is not going to make the mistake of meeting Pavel on all of these levels. She will, in fact, separate out the manageable, practical issues and address those. She quite rightly believes that two people can remain in conflict on several areas, such as their values or their interpretations of events, but still move forward on practical workplace issues. You do not have to share beliefs to work together.

Skylark does not care what Pavel thinks of black people or women generally, and she is not that concerned to argue or contradict Pavel's excuses or genuinely mitigating circumstances. She simply wants to learn from events and move the situation forward. So she invites Pavel's response on the checking system. When he launches into a defense, she asks him to stop, explaining that in the time they have she would much rather look at what they can learn and how to prevent it from happening again.

Pavel answers with a position: "Well, I suppose you will take me off recruitment."

GETTING PAVEL OUT OF THE CONFLICT ZONE

Skylark explores this position. "How would that improve the situation for you and me?"

Pavel replies, "It will be quick and tidy. I won't continuously feel under pressure."

He is adding issues here and Skylark refocuses him. "What would need to happen for you to feel that you could return to the level of excellence you attained before on recruitment?"

Pavel says, "I would like to feel competent and supported again."

Skylark now has an interest statement to work with. "Could you tell me what would need to happen for you to feel competent and supported again? The more specific the better."

Pavel responds, "No disrespect, love—you don't mind if I call you that do you? Some people are a bit funny about it—but I could do with you off my back!"

"I hear you, Pavel, but that is not an option. How else would you get back to feeling competent and supported? What type of support do you need?"

Because Skylark is not rising to any of the baits that Pavel has thrown her he becomes slightly withdrawn. This is not the response he expected. Skylark re-engages him by using the time constructively. "Pavel, it would be really useful for both of us to create some action points before we finish. I think we have seven or eight minutes left. Perhaps you can go away and think of some ways forward on the other issues, then we can meet again next week?"

Skylark is gradually motivating Pavel to trust her just a little, by remaining non-aggressive, open to his feelings, but also assertive around her own needs. They decide that he should stay on recruitment, but that all the timescales should be reviewed and some new checks instituted. Skylark is prepared to accept monthly one-to-one meetings (she wanted two every month) on the basis that this will give her a chance to support and develop Pavel, but will also reduce her need to check in with him almost every day.

At the end of the session Skylark asks Pavel for help in noting the action points, then requests feedback about their meeting, "to help her make sure that they have moved forward."

Pavel simply says, "It was not as uncomfortable as I thought."

Skylark sets up their first one-to-one meeting. Within days Pavel seems livelier, actually says good morning to Skylark when he sees her, and his work quickly returns to a good performance level. The work in the conflict zone has paid off. Pavel is also now capable of switching off some of their differences in order to get on.

KEY LEARNING POINTS

The mediation skills used in this example are:

- Getting the mediating manager out of the conflict zone.
- Setting the scene and building rapport.
- Reflective listening.
- Neutral language.
- Getting the other party out of the conflict zone.

CASE STUDY
MANAGING A VERY DIFFICULT CUSTOMER BY DEFUSING AGGRESSION AND NEEDS-BASED PROBLEM SOLVING

Customer service is a well-worn phrase. How good would your customer service be in the following situation? The mediating manager rises to the occasion, managing to offer excellent customer service under extreme pressure. This is the type of approach to customers that really impresses people. It contradicts all their expectations about cold, uncaring businesses.

Ted is manager of a large all-night supermarket that is part of a national chain. The company's policy is for managers to take their turn on the checkout so that they don't lose touch with their staff and customers.

    Nancy is a customer who has come in to buy some things for her new baby. She has her young children with her and has not had a good journey up and down the aisles. At the till the customer before her has trouble finding her credit cards, and then the till roll needs to be changed. Ted is fairly calm as Nancy approaches and unloads baby food, baby milk, and some feed-

Setting

ing bowls on to the conveyor. She then notices Ted's badge, prominently displaying "manager."

"On the TV it said you had Supadry nappies at half their normal price. 'Twice the dryness half the price,' that's what you said. There's no ******* [swear word deleted] Supadry nappies left, and your stacker tells me it will be days before you get some more. What are you doing advertising if you haven't got them on your shelves, you ******* cretins?"

DON'T GET SHOCKED, GET LISTENING

Ted is shocked, but fortunately remembers one of his mottoes as a mediating manager: "Don't get shocked, get listening." He pays attention, maintains open body language, and waits for a moment while Nancy continues.

"How am I supposed to get nappies for my children now? I've only got enough petrol to get home. You've really ****** it up for me." Nancy stares, awaiting a response.

GET MENTALLY INTO GEAR AND OPEN POSITIVELY

Now all eyes are on him and Nancy. Ted has a little mind game he plays to avoid responding provocatively under pressure. He quickly pictures a couple of provocative responses: "I'm not responsible for your children. The nappies I can deal with" or "Just because you've got noisy kids don't make my life a misery!" He then visualizes these being locked in a secure box and sent away. He takes a deep breath, relaxes his shoulders, and says instead, "Hello, I'm Ted, as you can see from my badge. So how can I help? Are you saying you haven't got what you came here for?"

DEFUSE, PAUSE, AND MOVE ON
Defuse and move on—Step 1

Nancy retorts, "I'm not leaving here until I've got some Supadry nappies. I don't care how you do it. This place is a ******* waste of time. Profit, that's all you care about."

Ted responds in a warm, positive tone. "Thank you for that feedback. I can see that we definitely have not met your expectations today. I am sure I can do something for you."

Nancy shouts. "Well, do something then, you moron!"

Ted replies, "OK, why don't I pack all your goods, get someone else on the till, then we can go to my office, or over there to the customer service desk, to sort something out for you?"

Create a pause and attend to people's needs

Nancy nods. Ted has already rang the bell for some staff help, and he gets the shopping off the conveyor, packed, and taken along with Nancy to the customer service area. He orders refreshments from the supermarket restaurant and brings them over with him, drinks for the children and their mother. This shows Nancy that he is at least paying her and her children attention on some level. Don't forget, aggression is often sustained, and sometimes escalates, if no attention is paid to people's needs.

Ted sits down by Nancy. "So I'm clear about what you want, you came in to buy Supadry nappies at the special price, but they are all gone. Understandably, you're not happy. You said you weren't going to leave until you got some Supadry nappies. Can we discuss how to fix you up with something now?"

Restart the conversation, go for dialogue not argument

Nancy stands up and starts waving her arms. "Do you think I'm stupid? A couple of drinks and sweet talking won't get my baby his nappies. I've only got enough money for Supadry."

"Madam," says Ted in a calm, neutral tone. "I can see this has made life very difficult for you. I am sure that I can sort something out. Could you sit down please?"

Defuse and move on—Step 2

Nancy does sit down, so Ted moves in with his opening offer. "You've only got enough money for Supadry. What if I gave you a pack of Babysweet—as you know, it's a top brand—at the Supadry price?" Ted knows that when faced with a rigid opponent he needs a powerful forward-moving gesture, but also that a number of linked offers are often as powerful as one grand gesture. He introduces the three parts of his "deal" incrementally, to convince Nancy that he is really trying to help.

Moving on: generating a range of options, creating a way forward with benefits for all

Nancy is not impressed with the first offer. "I've got used to Supadry."

"We can also put aside a couple of packs of Supadry for you when they come in tomorrow," adds Ted. Nancy is still not enthusiastic. Ted has one more move left, which is at no cost. He knows that there are stocks of Supadry but they have not yet reached the shelves. "OK, I can put aside a couple of packs of Supadry for you tomorrow after 4pm. If they do not come in by then you can have two packs free on your next visit."

Nancy finds this offer irresistible. Her concerns have been met fairly and squarely at low cost to the business. The benefits are also high. An angry customer now thinks more positively about the business, and all who witnessed this will be impressed too.

KEY LEARNING POINT

The mediation skills used in this case were:

- Don't get shocked, get listening.
- Get mentally into gear and open positively.
- Defuse, pause, and move on.
- Generate a wide range of linked options.

REFERENCES

1   Dixon, Nancy M (1998) *Dialogue at Work*, Lemos & Crane, London.
2   Fine, N & Macbeth, F (1992) *Playing with Fire*, LEAP, London.

11
Responding Constructively to the "Isms"

Some people who adopt inappropriate behavior at work shock us. We did not expect it from them. Others are more predictable, intentionally or unintentionally building up a track record of behavior that infringes other people's dignity and wellbeing, to varying degrees. They each pose their own problems and this chapter will help you manage two common examples: tackling the office sexist; and responding to a racist outburst about another manager.

There are two potential polarities present in situations involving this kind of "ism." First, they invite us either to join in or stand out: "You don't mind us saying this, do you?" or "Are you going to let them get away with that?" Group pressure is what sustains prejudice and discrimination. As a mediating manager you step outside that groupthink and stand for the things that connect people, not separate them: common values such as the need for respect, dignity, and recognition.

Secondly, when people witness or are confronted by other people's prejudices in action, their behavior falls into two distinct opposing patterns: fight—demand changes in behavior—or flight—avoid saying anything because of the discomfort it may cause. This chapter will help you take a detached but constructive, graduated response to oppressive behavior.

Ritual banter does serve a purpose in groups. It facilitates bonding and allows people to believe that they share common values. People often join in with banter because of the ritual, not because they agree with what it says. The risk, however, is that it helps the group to bond at a cost. Group banter works with very simple stereotypes, which demand adherence and allow lazy thinking. It is also exclusive and stifles diversity. Banter becomes difficult when new people join the group who may come from a different culture or have another visible difference, which may in the past have been the focus of banter.

CASE STUDY
TACKLING THE OFFICE SEXIST

Setting

Donal O'Flaherty is the HR manager of a large city solicitors' practice. Eight solicitors and Donal work in an open-plan office, with a pool of secretaries and administrative staff next door. Seven of the solicitors are men and all the administrative and secretarial staff are women.

Three months ago Jo Hyam, a 28-year-old woman, joined the team as a solicitor specializing in mediation and dispute resolution. This was a new venture for this firm, whose main business was commercial litigation, acquisitions, and mergers. Jo was fitting in very well with the team. She was fairly up-front in her views, but always took jibes and jokes in good humor. There was a strong after-work drinking culture in the office and Jo enjoyed coming to the pub. She looked relaxed and the section was starting to attract clients.

In the next three or four weeks Donal saw little of the team, as he was first on study leave finishing his professional qualification and then took annual holiday. On his return, he received an urgent email from Jo, asking to meet him. She was seriously thinking of resigning.

Donal arranged to meet Jo early one morning when the office is quiet and asked what had happened. Jo was hesitant to be specific initially, but soon got angry and upset. At this point she checked with him that this is a good time and place.

Donal said, "I want to listen, as you're clearly upset. To help you speak freely, let me say that at this stage I'm treating this as confidential."

Jo went on to tell him about a couple of incidents that caused her to feel "isolated and insulted, after all the hard work I put in to be accepted."

First, she received an email that one of the partners had cir-

culated to the team of lawyers. It referred to the upcoming appointment of a new secretary, since one was resigning. The email said, "Hopefully we'll get someone with legs right up to her arse, then at least we can have a bit more to look at than we had with Sadie [the woman who was leaving]." Jo had not said anything, which she now thinks may have been a mistake. It would seem she was being treated as an "honorary male," a phrase that had been used about her in the pub in jest. Donal had also seen this email, as he was part of the office group. He had not liked it much but had said nothing.

The key incident for Jo was when she walked in on a conversation in the coffee bar about women who become successful and their partners. A group of people were gathered round a newspaper containing photos of a popstar whose marriage had recently come to an end. The paper suggested that the marriage failed "because her husband could not get used to her being more successful than he was."

Sven, one of the senior solicitors who had been in the practice for 15 years, was being more salacious in his comments than the others, casually insulting a wide range of targets: "Any man who lets his wife take over the limelight must be a wimp" and "I bet she's a goer."

At one stage Sven turned to Jo and said, "I bet your old man isn't happy about you having a successful job, is he, love?"

Sven was generally viewed in the office as an amiable if somewhat irritating anachronism. At that moment Jo was no longer prepared to see Sven as in any way amiable. In fact, her partner spends his time at home looking after their children and there has been some friction between them. This particular round of banter was too close for comfort.

As the days passed after this incident, Jo noticed more and more derogatory comments about women, usually led by Sven and prefaced with a comment like "I'm not sexist, but…" or "I know you're not like this Jo, but…" She had become sensitized to the persistently sexist tone of many comments in the office. She felt she may be vulnerable if she raised these issues. Jo now wants Donal to do something, but not to mention her.

Donal is senior to the solicitors and responsible for HR practice, including the company values and code of practice. This *gives him authority in the area of inappropriate behavior from one staff member to another.*

Strategy

Donal is going to use a dual approach to managing this persistently inappropriate behavior:

- *Separate himself from the group by altering his own behavior.*
- *Use a menu of techniques to achieve behavior modification.*
- *Reset some of the boundaries around behavior for good.*

He is going to achieve this by:

- *Not participating personally in the inappropriate behavior.*
- *Being transparent about his goals.*
- *Responding to Sven as and when he uses inappropriate behavior.*
- *Using questions to break the flow.*
- *Checking the intention behind the behavior.*
- *Challenging constructively.*
- *Producing a series of steadily more challenging approaches if nothing changes.*
- *Signposting an intended modernization of corporate values and behavior.*

SUSTAINING RAPPORT

When over-used or applied in a mechanical, cold way, behavior and conversation management techniques can be irritating and may cause a temporary loss of rapport. Few people are comfortable with changing their behavior at someone else's behest. Do not forget that as a manager you have the right to lead, to exercise appropriate guidance, and, if necessary, to set limits to behavior. In this particular mediating manager mode, you may simply need to live with the discomfort you may experience and the hostility that may come your way. Signposting your intention, acknowledging feelings, and remaining assertive, rather than aggressive or manipulative, will significantly help you and others to manage these difficult interactions.

THE ONE-DOWN QUESTION

Groups that have been together for a while, like this group of solicitors, have often developed conversational conventions that seem like a code to an outsider. Stereotypical comments about others figure heavily in this code. They are not questioned or challenged. Everyone knows what they mean and that is comfortable. It is possible to interrupt this cosy group-think and eventually replace the code with something less negative.

The next time Donal hears one of those conversations about "busty women" or "crusty bids" (any woman who looks to be over 30), he asks a checking question, opting not to understand the code or buy into the stereotype. As far as he is concerned, when the derogatory code is used he is "one down," i.e., not understanding and seeking clarification. "So, who are we talking about here?" "Who do you mean?" Donal asks these questions persistently in a genuine tone of inquiry. A repeat of the phrase in a new derogatory comment gets the same treatment: "Yes, but who are you talking about?"

Sven sees Jo walking in the street as she approaches the office one morning and calls out, "Our bit of stuff is on her way."

Donal replies, "I know that you know who you're talking about, Sven, but as far as I am concerned that could mean anyone. Who are you talking about?"

"Come on, Donal, you know. Miss Wet-behind-the-ears, I don't think."

Donal persists, "Are you talking about Jo?" He carries on doing this until Sven realizes that his usual code is not working. He is not getting a bonding moment or an opening round of banter. His eventual response is to drop the negative term and simply not talk about Jo, so that he does not, in his words, "suffer a round of questions from the mad Irishman."

This technique works well with stereotypical comments generally. For example:

- A colleague says, "I see that invoicing have taken on a couple of Pakis." You reply, "Are they from Pakistan?"
- A manager says, "He's got to be a poof." You reply, "Who do you mean?" or "Who are you saying is gay?"

All you are seeking here is a name, a neutral description of someone, rather than an oppressive label. If the one-down question does not work, ask for people's names to be put back into the conversation.

Sven: "That really tarty one from reception smiled at me today."
Donal: "Do you mean Rachel?"

REDIRECTING QUESTIONS

Redirecting questions are more active than one-down questions. They are seeking to move a speaker away from negative comments and looking for the intention behind these.

Donal walks into the coffee room and Sven is complaining to other staff about a female cleaner. As usual, no one interrupts. "Don't get me wrong, I love colored people, but she could barely speak English. I hope she is at least good on her back, eh chaps, because her cleaning is certainly rubbish."
   Donal walks up to Sven. "Sven, what were you saying about Adelia? Is this a work issue?"
   Sven: "What are you getting so shirty about, old lad?"
   Donal: "It sounded like you were concerned about the cleaning. Or were you just passing comment on the cleaner's color?" Once again the tone here is crucial. Donal is checking whether Sven is simply expressing a derogatory opinion or has a valid work concern. So the question needs to be asked in a calm, inquisitive tone.
   Sven: "Don't get me wrong, Donal, I've got a lot of time for these foreign types. You've got to admit she's a bit of a no-hoper that one!"
   Donal: "I'm just hearing negative comments here, Sven. What exactly are you trying to achieve here? Is this some sort of complaint?"
   Sven: "Forget it, Donal." He walks away.

CHALLENGE CONSTRUCTIVELY

Up to now Donal's actions have primarily been to let Sven know that the latter's opinions are not shared. He is signaling that he is not in this collective club that talks others down. One or two other people are also detaching themselves from that part of the group interaction. Donal now intends to move into more chal-

lenging mode if necessary. He does not have to wait long for an opportunity.

During a staff meeting there is a prolonged discussion about developing new business. Sven has prepared a PowerPoint presentation that has several indirectly sexist ingredients. All the visuals include men, he constantly refers to his colleagues as "guys," uses anecdotes about male-dominated sports, and always uses "he" when talking about potential competitors. Sven's banter with the group, which includes the female admin team, is punctuated by the usual "darling," "love," and "dear" for the women, and first names for the men. He also routinely picks out male members of the group to ask questions or respond, and gives great praise to male contributions while barely paying attention to the women.

When entering into challenge mode it is as well to remember why you are doing so. What strikes Donal is that Sven's whole approach is centered on some extremely limited assumptions about men, women, families, and so on. Donal is not driven by political correctness or personal indignation, but by sound business sense. Sven's exclusive, limiting approach demonstrates a mind trapped in clichés and unaware of a changing world. This is what he wants to get across when challenging Sven.

*Donal uses the DESC sequence (see page 134). "Sven, I've sat and listened for 20 minutes and I haven't heard one response from the women in the room [**D**escribe the behavior in neutral language]. I think we're really missing an opportunity if we don't involve everyone [**E**xplain the effect on you]. I imagine you were going to go on to that [**S**how understanding of the intention behind the behavior], so could you get some responses from female colleagues soon [**C**ommunicate an alternative]?"*

This is a very specific challenge and Sven begrudgingly follows Donal's advice. As the responses come back, Sven pays little attention.

In the final round of dialogue, Donal makes another, more strategic challenge. "What I have also noticed is that you are talking as though the world is full of men alone. I feel uncomfortable at focusing so heavily on men, which limits the business opportunity. I understand that is what you are familiar with, but I personally would like some ideas about working in different areas, with women in business and the home. What does the group think about this?"

Donal is aware that this may set him on a collision course with Sven, so he stays in the room after the presentation and asks him for an urgent chat. The two men sit down in Donal's office and Sven is very angry. Donal listens to Sven, "on condition that Sven then listens to him."

EXCHANGE INFORMATION IN THE CONFLICT ZONE

Sven: "You're determined to make me look a fool, laddie, I can see that. First that coffee room business, now disrupting my presentation. What's it all about? Are you some kind of politically correct campaigner? I haven't worked here for 15 years to be made look a fool in front of the girls; sorry, I suppose I should call them ladies, or women, or whatever the right word is."

Donal: "This isn't personal for me, Donal, it's practical. You're right, we do have very different ideas. I'm a fan of including and involving people, I'm bored by seeing women in one group and men in another. I think it's limiting and I'm annoyed by it. My behavior toward you has been for a purpose, though. With all your experience and knowledge, I expect you to know when you are excluding people or potentially upsetting them. Haven't you noticed how people react to you?"

Sven: "Well, no one has actually said a word to me about my behavior. I am and always have been very popular with the ladies."

SIGNPOST POLICY AND VALUES

Donal: "What I am asking for, Sven, is more care in the future. Some of the words and phrases you use, like 'busty tart' and 'girlies'—do you think they are respectful?"

Sven: "No one pays attention to that. The staff are fine about it."

Donal: "They may be now, Sven, but we have a new code of conduct that talks about respect and equality. The idea is that you use words that signal a positive attitude to all kinds of people. I know we used a lot of slang, but it can be sloppy. Some people misunderstand it."

Eventually Sven hears Donal's point. Donal can do no more informally. He does get Sven to think about the strategic benefits of modifying his behavior: "There are many important female players out there, Sven. How do you feel about the fact that key account holders will want a modern, positive approach?"

Sven is quiet now, feeling weighed down. He is beginning to realize that Donal does have the authority to set limits, but he is not happy. In order to close constructively, Donal asks Sven to go back over what has been said to check clarity. Donal makes it clear that this is not about Sven's work and that everyone will eventually need to demonstrate a new awareness of issues such as this. This type of interaction rarely ends comfortably. Donal sets up a follow-up date to continue the discussion.

KEY LEARNING POINTS

The mediation skills used in this case include:

- Sustaining rapport.
- One-down and redirecting questions.
- Challenging constructively.
- Exchanging information in the conflict zone.
- Signposting policy and values.

CASE STUDY
MANAGING A SUDDEN RACIST OUTBURST

I am sometimes surprised by the oppressive views and language that can suddenly and randomly tumble from the mouths of strangers, colleagues, and friends. We have devised six steps to help manage these interactions.

CHECKLIST
STEPS FOR MANAGING A RACIST OUTBURST

1 Listening through.
2 Talking through.
3 Influence and persuasion.
4 Establishing groundrules.
5 Challenging behavior constructively.
6 Closing constructively.

Setting

Mahmood meets fellow manager Melanie to talk about restructuring their department. All departments have been asked to come up with cost-cutting proposals. Mahmood likes Melanie, who is efficient and energetic. Midway through the meeting Mahmood becomes aware of a shift of tone as Melanie speaks about one of her staff.

STEP 1: LISTENING THROUGH

■ Give space and reflect.
■ Use open questions.
■ Pay attention.
■ Acknowledge feelings.
■ Allow feelings to be vented.
■ Reflect neutrally.

Melanie: "Derek, you know, the Jamaican guy on my team. He's got such a chip on his shoulder. He is surly, difficult, and generally unhelpful. I think I got a raw deal, getting one of those on my team."

Would you have interrupted by now? The idea of this approach is to listen, test the tone, and allow feelings to be vented—until you think you might be giving the impression of collusion or agreement.

Mahmood is shocked, particularly as he thought Melanie was tolerant. He asks an open question to move Melanie on: "Why don't you tell me more about Derek?"

Melanie continues: "Well, he comes in, lazes around, loves the sound of his own voice, probably drives a BMW, although he can't afford one. You know the kind of thing."

Melanie seems to be getting into a negative groove, so Mahmood thinks it is time to acknowledge feelings, summarize neutrally, and move on to step 2.

STEP 2: TALKING THROUGH

■ Use clarifying questions.
■ Acknowledge feelings and set aside.
■ Check whether there are any issues behind the opinions.

Mahmood: "So Derek is having quite a negative effect on you. You think he has a negative attitude to work. What makes you say that?"

Melanie pauses. "You only have to look at him. He's got through college without any effort. No one really challenges Jamaican men, do they? He's had it easy, so he coasts."

Mahmood: "I am hearing your feelings about Derek, Melanie, and some general thoughts about Jamaican men. Could we concentrate on his work? Talk to me about examples of his work, good or bad."

- ■ Explain your role.
- ■ Model fairness and equality.
- ■ Check what people want out of the discussion.
- ■ Encourage people to reflect on their behavior.

Melanie is still making comments about Derek. She feels strongly about the way he "stands over her," "walks into her room," "speaks over people," and "plays loud music on his minidisk player at breaks."

Mahmood explains: "I'm not here to judge Derek or you, Melanie. My experience of Derek is quite different from yours. How is what you are saying relevant to our discussion about cost saving?"

Melanie: "We've got to get rid of some people, haven't we? Why not cut away the dead wood first?"

Mahmood: "How about we focus on the general staffing issue and work out some objective criteria for the staff we want to keep and the type we may need to let go?"

For a while Melanie goes along with that suggestion. They work on criteria for staffing, such as competencies, experience, and length of service.

- ■ Establish groundrules and clarify that people understand.
- ■ Ask people to work to the groundrules.

Suddenly Melanie goes back to the subject of Derek. "You know, the other day Derek came in with one of his mates, and they had so much gold on them together that they could have opened a

STEP 3:
INFLUENCE AND
PERSUASION

STEP 4:
ESTABLISHING
GROUNDRULES

jewelry shop. Where does he get the money from for that?"

Mahmood moves into more directive mode. He wants to re-focus Melanie's attention. "Melanie, Derek seems to be very present in this conversation again. I can understand he is taking a lot of your energy right now. Can we focus on general criteria, not individual staff?"

STEP 5: CHALLENGING BEHAVIOR CONSTRUCTIVELY

DESCRIBE
■ the behavior in neutral language.
EXPLAIN
■ the effect of the behavior on you.
SHOW UNDERSTANDING
■ recognize the feelings and intention behind the behavior.
COMMUNICATE
■ a preferred alternative.

Melanie is upset, and feeling under pressure. She now turns on Mahmood. "That's the trouble with you lot. You all stick together. I should have known better."

Mahmood: "Melanie, when you spend a lot of time speaking about Derek's failings, I find it hard to work with you on the restructuring issue. I know he's at the forefront of your mind, but I would rather not hear about any individual staff right now."

This refocuses Melanie. If this had not achieved the desired effect—to change Melanie's behavior speedily, without blaming her—Mahmood could have moved on to the next step.

STEP 6: CLOSING CONSTRUCTIVELY

■ Give a final warning.
■ Take a break, giving a reason for the break.
■ Leave a way back into the discussion if possible.
■ Stop the session.

12

Investigating Sensitive Issues

Roberto has been asked by Amelia to investigate her concerns about Pietro. He catches her in the corridor and asks her to "tell me about the argument you had with Pietro when you say he verbally abused you."

She replies that it was not an argument; Pietro had shouted at her.

Roberto asks, "What did you do to make him so mad?"

"I did nothing," Amelia retorts. "He is always crazy and angry."

Roberto feels uncomfortable and checks, "Are you always so negative about the men around here?"

This causes Amelia to respond defensively, "What are you getting at? I'm not negative about men. Pietro just finds women like me threatening."

Roberto replies, "Well, you are pretty scary. Ease off. I'm sure Pietro doesn't mean anything. In fact, I know he rather fancies you."

"Nothing," thinks Amelia, "could be further from the truth."

Literature and the media have given us many images of investigators at work, particularly criminal investigators. The bumbling Clouseau, the raincoat-clad, charismatically challenged Columbo, the inscrutable Charlie Chan, and Sherlock Holmes—mainly men searching and analyzing, each pursuing the truth in his own way. We remember them for their character, their style, or lack of it. But what do they actually do and do they do it well?

Investigators like working with facts, analyzing information, forming hypotheses of what might have happened, identifying suspects, and then collecting information to prove their theories. The most celebrated investigators rarely get it wrong and almost always "get their man."

Many manager investigators also see themselves as crusaders seeking the truth, intellectuals pursing a hypothesis, or seducers wooing people into confessions. They will use any method to get to the bottom of a situation, including intimidation, manipulation, and entrapment. They may get results, but TV investigators are not good models for investigating managers. More mundane virtues such as rigor, persistence, and focus are far more helpful to managers when they are investigating complaints, grievances, and other sensitive issues. Investigators also need to be very clear about the boundaries of their role.

FINDING OUT OR COMING OUT WITH FINDINGS?

The real purpose of an investigation is to find out what has been, and in some cases still is, happening. Each investigation requires the application of search and analysis techniques and the drawing together of information. It helps if investigators are given a well-defined brief and a clear indication of what they are looking for.

Often managers find themselves in situations where they are also expected to adjudicate: assess information; confirm or deny a version of events; judge a type of behavior; or evaluate what degree of seriousness is attached to a situation or series of events. Provided that the activities of investigation and adjudication are kept separate, a manager can perform both roles, for example if a customer complains about the delivery of an order or a staff member complains about a missing payslip.

The manager **receives** the complaint and **explores** the situation by talking to and listening to people and looking at records. Next the manager **assesses** the information, setting what was promised against what was received or not; comparing the various versions of events; making judgments about credibility; and putting the information in context by using previous experience or written guidelines. Managers investigating formally, and often informally, will also **respond**, by presenting and discussing their findings with the complainant, and in some cases the other people involved; directing the customer toward a solution; negotiating a way forward; and setting up a review process if necessary.

The feedback we have received from investigators, and people who have been involved in investigations, is that the process and the rapport with the parties are often damaged and the outcomes tainted by people moving into judgment mode too early. This makes a sensitive situation worse in two ways:

- **Inadequate collection of information**—the investigator stops exploring, convinced that they already know the truth, and only pays attention to information that backs up their judgment. Other significant information is ignored when received because it does not fit the conclusion they are drawing; what could be vital information is never sought because only certain avenues of inquiry are considered still open.
- **Self-perpetuating low levels of rapport and negative conversation management**—an investigator who, thinking that someone is guilty of bullying, asks them leading questions and interrupts their pleas for mitigation shouldn't be surprised when the party gets angry and challenging. The investigator who reacts defensively to the party's frustration may find the party getting angrier and aggressive. It is all too easy to conclude that the party must be guilty of bullying: just look at the way they have behaved to a neutral investigator. The more and the earlier you judge, the further you get from the truth.

WHAT MAKES A GOOD INVESTIGATOR?

This chapter explores how mediation skills can assist in all four stages of an investigation: receiving, exploring, assessing, and responding. The key mediation skills in an investigative context are:

- Reflective listening and questioning techniques.
- Conversation management.
- Neutrality and impartiality.

What also comes from mediation is the ability to design and run a fair, rigorous, and transparent process.

CASE STUDY
IS THIS BULLYING?

Setting

Manjit Kaur had been given a car park space at her office, due to her rheumatoid arthritis. However, when she was moved to another office within the same building, she was told that the car park space was needed for official use. Her new manager, Sara Ito, also began to criticize her for taking too many breaks, working late without supervision, and, twice a week, taking long lunch breaks.

Manjit argued that she started work late as her disability made her very slow in the mornings and twice a week at lunchtime she went swimming to loosen her limbs. This had been OK with her previous manager, but the new regime seemed much less understanding. After a while Manjit also heard that her appraisal reports indicated that she was a loner who had difficulty in relating to others, and that her relationships at work were not that good. She was described by Sara as "not a team player, who expected others to adapt to her ways."

Sara had been told by her own manager to get more out of the team and was taking a tough line with everyone. She had found it almost impossible to speak to Manjit, who was not responding to emails requesting a meeting between them. Whenever Sara felt there were problems in the team she got them all together, to talk the issues through. Manjit found this intimidatory. Manjit was also very upset that Sara had promised to push for a new car park space and had set up a meeting with the facilities manager, but at the last minute it had been canceled. The day after Manjit had gone to talk to Sara, but Sara

was on the phone and was not interested in talking it through.
Manjit was frustrated and stormed out, unsure what to do next.

Many people who feel they are being harassed, bullied, or discriminated against are reluctant to report their experience for a number of reasons: fear that it might rebound on them (particularly if the behavior is escalating); lack of faith in the remedies available; or doubts about themselves—"Can this really be happening?" or "What might I be doing to contribute to this?"

There have for many years been a number of conventional points of contact in many organizations, where someone can go if they feel that a colleague is behaving inappropriately, denying them opportunities, or having a significantly negative effect on their work. The usual options are to take the issue up with the person directly involved; tell their line manager; speak with a member of the human resources team; or go to an occupational health professional, staff counselor, trade union representative, friend, or colleague.

A range of workplaces in both the private and public sectors have set up teams of trained contact officers, harassment support officers, or colleague support network members. They are recruited from a broad cross-section of the organization and their names and roles are widely publicised. Initial monitoring suggests that they are being widely used as the first point of contact and are performing two important roles:

■ Creating an effective listening service, which is helping staff to feel acknowledged and, in some cases, empowered to manage their situation more effectively themselves.
■ Helping people to assess what options are available to them and how to address sometimes complex, sensitive situations.

POINTS OF CONTACT

KEY LEARNING POINTS

A range of different points of contact should be available to create a safe, effective complaint-receiving capacity. Boundaries and groundrules need to be made clear at the earliest opportunity, particularly clarifying the degree of confidentiality surrounding allegations of bullying, harassment, and discrimination.

Anyone designated as a potential point of contact, particularly a manager, should be able to use reflective listening skills, explore the issues fully, and make an initial neutral assessment of the issues with the complainant. Many vulnerable people are exasperated by the apparently dismissive approach initially taken to their issues. Good listening and a full exploration of the options are imperative at this early stage.

INTERVIEWING THE COMPLAINANT

Receiving the grievance, using reflective listening and open questions, and conversation management

Manjit calls in unexpectedly on Oliver, the HR manager. She says she needs to talk and looks distressed. "It's about Sara."

Oliver checks that it is OK to shut his office door and phones a colleague to advise that he is not available for an hour. He puts his phone on voicemail and starts by briefly setting the scene, then moves into listening mode with an open question. "I'm keen to hear what you have to say and I want to let you know that at this stage this is confidential. Once you have told me what's going on we can look at what to do about it. So describe in your own words, Manjit, what has been happening."

Manjit starts in a rush, pouring out her distress and describing a number of significant events.

Oliver occasionally uses conversation management to influence Manjit to work to a structure, exploring all the issues, events and feelings first, then assessing and responding. "I can see that you're very upset, Manjit, and I can assure you that there are many ways I can help, but I will find it much easier to look at ways of helping when you have told me everything that you think is important."

After about 40 minutes of talking Manjit is still upset, but feels acknowledged by Oliver, so she now signals that she would like

to know where to go from here, and who could help.

Oliver reflects back the significant events, acknowledges her feelings, and then tries to clarify and map out the broad complaint. "You are unhappy with Sara's behavior toward you, and every time you have tried to let her know, in your words she has 'been dismissive and turned it on you.' You believe that she has singled you out for unfair treatment, refuses to acknowledge your special needs, and gives you nothing but negative feedback. You do not think things will improve without outside help."

Manjit confirms that this is an accurate summary.

Oliver needs to explore what Manjit wants out of this situation first, to give him a flavor of her level of expectation and degree of need. This will help him later, when assessing options and deciding a way forward.

KEY LEARNING POINT

It is tempting at the early stage of hearing a complaint to race ahead and explain the options, but getting some sense of what the complainant wants before you do this will help to assess options and respond effectively. If you haven't got enough information to assess the way forward, more probing questions will also be necessary to complete the exploratory phase of the investigation.

- **Timescale questions**—"When did this start? What is the most recent incident? What happened in between?"
- **Critical incident questions**—"You mentioned the situation at the staff meeting. Give me some background. How were you feeling before you went into the meeting? What sort of day had you had? What happened next? Could you describe your reaction and other people's reactions? How did this leave you feeling? Is there anything else you want to tell me about what happened at that meeting?"
- **Specifying questions**—"When you say..., what do you mean? Could you give me an example?" These are how, what, where, and when questions.

Useful probing questions for building up detail

Neutral assessment of
situations

Bullying and harassment are notoriously difficult to assess and respond to effectively. We have learned two main things from mediation that are also helpful in investigations:

■ Don't make judgments until you have collected all the information you can.
■ Seek objective criteria for assessment, against which to make and explain your judgments.

There are many indicators to look for in situations involving allegations of bullying and harassment:

■ **Behavior**—is this behavior that could be identified as bullying?
■ **Impact**—what effect is this having on the complainant and on others?
■ **Mitigation**—could anything add to the understanding of why this might be going on? Are there any specific circumstances that may be contributing? Is there anything that the complainant might be doing that is contributing to this?
■ **Corroboration**—could other people confirm the allegations? Has anyone else seen or experienced the same or similar behavior?
■ **Intention**—was the alleged behavior deliberate? Has an explanation been sought from the person described as a bully? Has the other person signaled why this behavior is being adopted?

CHECKLIST
EXAMPLES OF BULLYING BEHAVIOR

- Finding fault in work when none exists.
- Personalizing work criticism.
- Persistently criticizing.
- Making personal attacks.
- Misuse of power or authority.
- Denying recognition or rewards.
- Denying opportunities.

CHECKLIST
EFFECTS OF BULLYING IN THE WORKPLACE

- Loss of concentration or focus.
- Demotivation.
- Feelings of anxiety or fear.
- Reduction of skill levels.
- Reduced performance.
- Altered participation in teams.
- Stress.
- Deterioration in mental or physical health.

Once Oliver has listened and gathered all the information Manjit wants to give, another phase of the conversation is initiated. In this phase Oliver will ask probing questions, so that he can get the information he needs to assess the situation. This transition from open, reflective listening to a more probing style needs to be managed sensitively. Oliver has already summarized in detail and kept notes, with Manjit's permission, although they are yet to decide what will happen to the notes.

"Thanks for being so open, Manjit. How are you doing so far?"

Manjit says that she wants to know what Oliver can do. Oliver has recognized in Manjit's account a number of incidents in which Sara's behavior, as described, bears the hallmarks of bullying. The negative impact on Manjit personally is tangible and she has alluded to a number of significantly negative consequences of Sara's behavior on her work. On this basis alone, Oliver is convinced that this situation needs attention. The question is: What sort of attention would be most appropriate? Manjit has already said that she wants it to stop and "if necessary she will go all the way to stop it." Oliver clarified that, and Manjit explained that she was prepared to take out a formal grievance, if necessary.

To give her the best possible advice and support, Oliver explained that he had a few more questions that would help determine the best way forward. He wanted to check if Manjit needed a break, and she said that she could do with a glass of water but declined to take a break. Oliver let his colleague know that he would need another 30 minutes undisturbed, and he and Manjit continued their conversation.

KEY LEARNING POINT

After getting a full, free account of the situation in the speaker's own words, investigators should bear in mind the information they need to collect in order to enable effective, neutral assessment of situations, and to ask targeted, rather than random, unplanned questions. Checklists of questions like this can be built up over time and used as prompts, provided that they are not introduced into conversations mechanically and in an interrogative tone.

Useful probing questions for allegations of bullying and harassment

■ **Impact**
   — "What effect is this having on you personally, your work, and your relationships with colleagues?"
   — "How were you feeling about your job/manager/colleagues before this?"
   — "How are you feeling now?"
   — "Could you give me some specific examples of how your work has been affected?"

■ **Previous attempts to move the situation on**
   — "Have you spoken to him/her directly about this?"
   — "Have you spoken to anyone else about this?"
   — "Describe what happened. What effect did that have?"

■ **Mitigation**

— "Are there any specific circumstances that may be contributing to his/her behavior?"

— "Is there anything you are doing that may be contributing to the situation?"

■ **Corroboration**

— "Has anyone else seen or experienced the same or similar behavior?"

■ **Intention**

— "Has he or she ever explained the way s/he manages you/others?"

— "Is there any reason you can think of why the manager's behavior toward you appears much harsher than his or her management style toward others?"

— "When you raised issues with your manager, what was his/her reaction? What reason did s/he give for the behavior?"

Detailed information gathering is now complete and Oliver has earmarked 15 minutes to look at options, because he feels that he has sufficient information to do this.

Neutral assessment of options

Where possible this process should be conducted openly and transparently with the complainant, working out the most appropriate way forward on the basis of the following factors.

CHECKLIST
FACTORS AFFECTING THE OUTCOME OF AN INVESTIGATION

■ **The degree of vulnerability of the complainant**—level of distress, level of current support, emotional and psychological condition, special needs, stress and health levels. (In some cases it may take more time and need other professional skills to assess this factor.)

■ **What the complainant wants**—a win/win or win/lose solution, resolution or vindication, formal or informal approach, speedy or gradual approach.

■ **The nature of the allegations**—degree of seriousness, amount of specific information, number of instances, frequency, pattern.

> ■ **The capacity of the organization to act**—who is available to offer support, assist negotiation, mediate, investigate, adjudicate? How soon?
> ■ **The constraints on the organization**—procedural guidelines, resource limits, legal rights and duties.

Oliver wants to respond as positively and realistically as he can and talks Manjit through various options. He is in favor of mediation, but Manjit is not.

Oliver: "So you've made it clear that you want Sara to change her behavior toward you significantly, for her to recognize your disability and allow you to work more flexibly. You added that you are not looking for special favors. The situation is affecting your health and self-confidence but you do not want to go off sick, or lose your job, which you used to enjoy so much. We have some internal trained mediators who I am sure could help here." Oliver gives a brief outline of mediation and its benefits.

Manjit: "I do not trust her, you know. She is too devious. I want someone to look into this. I'll be talking to my union rep. They are encouraging all staff to take a firm line in these types of situations and not to let management walk all over us."

So what are the options? In their organization Oliver can offer an informal investigation, conducted by him, or a formal investigation carried out by a senior manager from another department. In an informal investigation Oliver would work out the terms of reference with Manjit, particularly about talking to witnesses and whether or not to conduct an interview with Sara. The interviews would be thorough, confidential, and structured, like this one with Manjit. Clearly, the potential for some discomfort initially becomes greater the broader the remit of the informal investigation. Discreet interviews with other team members are proposed, but no contact with Sara at this stage.

The formal option will take longer and involve a series of interviews with Manjit first, witnesses as required, and Sara. Sara would need a preview of the allegations before she was interviewed. Detailed notes would be taken and signed off by the interviewee, and a full written report would be compiled and submitted to a panel for consideration.

A FORMAL INVESTIGATION

Manjit decides to take a break to get advice, to speak to her partner, her trade union representative, and her parents. Oliver works up a final outline summary of key incidents and issues and confirms it with Manjit, and she agrees for this to be used as an outline to prepare any future investigator.

A week later Manjit requests, in writing, a formal investigation, and the written complaint and Oliver's summary are passed on to Phoebe, a senior manager from another region, who has no prior knowledge of either principal party.

There are a number of possible findings at the end of a formal investigation into bullying, each of which can assist when considering different types of action. Table 17 is a simplified version of what might be suggested under different circumstances.

Table 17 Findings and outcomes of a formal investigation

Findings	**Types of action suggested**
Not proven—the bullying did not happen.	Support for complainant, monitoring future events.
Partially proven—the bullying happened but the bully was unaware of the impact of his/her behavior.	Support for complainant and person complained about (in order to achieve raised awareness and behavioral change).
Proven—the bullying happened and the perpetrator should have been aware of the impact of his/her behavior.	Disciplinary action against person complained about.
Insufficient evidence.	No action.
Complaint made maliciously.	Action against the complainant.

KEY LEARNING POINT

Map out in advance what type of information would point to the different types of findings. This will help in the adjudication process. Some examples include:

- The investigator's report outlines five witnesses who have seen the manager making repeated suggestive remarks to his secretary, despite requests not to. Likely outcome—proven.
- The investigator's report outlines a series of difficult incidents mostly confirmed by the complainant and the person complained about. The manager says that she was just doing her job, the complainant says that she was picked on. Performance records show a considerable fall-off in performance levels prior to the alleged incidents. Finding—partially proven.

CREATING A FAIR, RIGOROUS PROCESS

Formal investigations can also benefit from some ingredients of the interactive mediation approach. The following is the structure we work to when we conduct an investigation, and we aim for fairness, transparency, and rigor throughout.

Set-up

- Let the principal parties know in writing who you and any investigating team are and how the investigation will work.
- Include in this levels of confidentiality, timescales, rights of representation and support, and possible outcomes.
- Create a schedule of interviews, on private, neutral territory if possible.

Interviewing the complainant

- Set the scene, describe the process, clarify groundrules, check understanding and willingness.
- Initiate a "free account" using open questions and the funnel technique (see pages 69) to gather information.
- Summarize in detail.
- Start probing and seeking information that will help assess the situation.
- Summarize in detail.
- Check for witnesses.
- Explain the continuing process, particularly that for signing

off notes of the session.

■ Create a brief overview, to be used to inform the person complained about of key incidents and issues.

■ Set the scene, describe the process, clarify groundrules, check understanding and willingness.

Interviewing the person complained about

■ Outline the key incidents and issues as described by the complainant and get a detailed response.

■ Initiate a "free account" of their version of events using open questions and the funnel technique to gather information.

■ Summarize in detail.

■ Start probing and seeking information that will help assess the situation.

■ Summarize in detail.

■ Check for witnesses.

■ Explain the continuing process, particularly that for signing off notes of the session.

■ Clarify the role of the witness and the groundrules and check understanding and willingness to continue.

Interviewing witnesses

■ Ask them to describe what they know.

■ Probe and clarify.

■ Summarize in detail.

■ Explain the continuing process, particularly that for signing off notes of the session.

■ Check the information gathered and go back to people for more detail if necessary.

Reporting

■ Compile a report, including an introduction and overview of the issues and the investigation process; the complaint, the response, additional evidence, findings, conclusions (if required), and appendices (including signed statements).

The most difficult part of this process is often the interview with the person alleged to have used bullying behavior. Mediation skills can help to manage this interaction, as the snapshots below demonstrate.

BUILDING RAPPORT AND MAINTAINING NEUTRALITY UNDER PRESSURE

Sara is not pleased about this investigation and puts the investigator, Phoebe, under a great deal of pressure from the start. "What sort of fiction is this? Me, a bully? She's a nightmare. Lazy and disruptive. I cannot believe you are giving credence to her whingeing."

Phoebe replies neutrally but warmly, "You may want to say more about that later, Sara. I can see you've got strong feelings about Manjit. But for the moment can I just explain our frame of reference for this investigation?"

Sara listens but looks stressed, so Phoebe starts with basic introductions. "I'm Phoebe Radlinsky, Manager of Distribution in the South East, and I have been brought in to investigate allegations against you by Manjit Kaur, a member of your team. This is Stephen Boateng, my note taker. I will be asking all the questions, but I may bring Stephen in occasionally to remind us of what has been said so far. Could you say a little about your history and role in the organization?"

Sara does.

"Thanks for that, Sara. How are you feeling?"

Sara shrugs. "Embarrassed and angry."

Phoebe goes on to ask, "Are there any questions you would like to ask about the process today?"

Sara replies, "Yes, why invest all these resources in such a frivolous allegation?"

Phoebe again remains neutral. "Your concerns about resources are shared by all of us, Sara. We aim, as an organization, to take allegations of bullying seriously. You will get every chance to respond to Manjit's allegations shortly and also to tell your own version of events."

Sara is still looking agitated as Phoebe outlines the process. She tells Sara that she will be going through each allegation, using an outline supplied by Manjit, and will be looking for a response from Sara. Sara's anger has not put Phoebe on the defensive. She has dealt with it in a quietly acknowledging way, while maintaining impartiality and the integrity of the process.

DEFUSING AGGRESSION AND DRAWING OUT ISSUES

One of the critical incidents in this scenario is the meeting between Sara and Manjit, scheduled to discuss why Manjit's parking place had been taken away. Sara admitted that she had not been there and that they had had an angry exchange about it the next day. Her version was very different from Manjit's. She was scathing about Manjit: "She marched into my office with her stick and came right up to my desk. I was on the phone, so she stood there tapping her stick agitatedly on the floor, like some kind of idiot, and when I was off the phone told me in no uncertain terms that I was discriminating against her because of her disability. Disability indeed. My mother has got arthritis and she can barely move. Manjit really piles on the agony. I am not prepared to put up with such flagrant displays of disrespect from one of my team. She is a lazy, selfish slacker."

Phoebe pauses Sara to say, "Sara, I can hear you feel indignant about this, but when you describe Manjit in those terms I do not get any idea about how you were managing Manjit. Perhaps if you could concentrate on that? [DESC sequence] How did you manage this situation and Manjit afterwards?"

"Well, if she had listened to me for a minute or two, she would have found out something to her advantage. I had actually spoken to Terry, my boss, about getting another parking space for Manjit and he was very hopeful. After that meeting I immediately withdrew my request."

Phoebe uses a probing question. "So how would you evaluate your handling of that situation, in retrospect?"

Sara replies, "I would do the same again. You can't let people get away with that, can you?"

Sara responds to all the complaints, agreeing that some things happened as Manjit claimed, but stressing that her intention was to move Manjit along, get her working with the team, and generally "give her a kick up the backside," as in Sara's view she was coasting.

Phoebe gets Stephen, the note taker, to summarize, and then uses signposting and the funnel technique to get Sara's sense of the background to this complaint. "I would like now to get your perspective of working with Manjit. Talk me through your working relationship with Manjit. What issues does this situation raise for you?"

GIVING THE PERSON COMPLAINED ABOUT SPACE TO GIVE THEIR VERSION OF EVENTS

NEUTRAL QUESTIONS

The questions used by Oliver, outlined in the earlier informal investigation, are good examples of neutral questions in that they were non-blaming and needed to be asked to enable a more objective assessment of the situation. Useful neutral questions for the person alleged to have used bullying behavior are:

- *"How would you describe your management style and how you used it on Manjit?"*
- *"Have you ever talked to her about your working relationship and the way you are managing her?"*
- *"What approach do you take to other team members? What type of feedback do you give them? What feedback do you get from other team members about your behavior toward them?"*
- *"What is your experience of working with staff with special needs? How would you describe the way you worked? What is your approach to special needs, such as a person's periodic lack of physical mobility?"*
- *"What sort of a manager would you say you are? What do others say about you?"*

CLOSING CONSTRUCTIVELY

Because such a careful, neutral approach was taken in this case, a progressive resolution was possible. The finding was that Sara had not taken enough account of Manjit's disability, but that she had not intentionally bullied her. Some disability awareness training was provided for Sara and a mentor manager set up for her. Special provision was made for Manjit to work flexible hours, but under Sara's supervision.

The identity of the person who arrives at this conclusion will depend on the organization's terms of reference. Some companies have a nominated independent person or complaints coordinator who will receive formal complaints, assign an investigator(s), and be the back-stop for, and custodian of, the process.

Another option is to refer all formal complaints to a panel that sets up an investigation and adjudicates on it. In this model, investigators not only provide assistance with debriefing but will always attend face-to-face debriefs, where possible and appropriate, to help adjudicators explain their findings. Debriefing sessions create a final, personal opportunity to achieve the most constructive close possible.

The head of HR who commissioned the investigation set up separate personal debriefs for Manjit and Sara. The details of their findings and the reasons for them were outlined. Responses were heard and the participants were given a feedback form for completion within a week, which asked a few simple questions to evaluate the investigation process, including "Was the process as expected? How? How fair was the investigator on a scale of 1–10? What other comments would you make about the investigation?"

The parties were not overjoyed, but then grievances rarely end with positive feelings. This is one reason why taking an early mediation-style approach can help everyone to avoid longer-term misery. Changing the culture of the organization so that mediation is more acceptable to staff can go a long way toward helping them to avoid unhappy endings.

Manjit was pleased that her issues were validated, but was unsure about Sara's "punishment." Sara felt let down: She was upset that she had to receive extra training and initially felt insulted about the mentor. Neither party appealed and they continued to work in the same team. Their relationship was frosty, but as Manjit's work came back up to the standard it had been at before the grievance, Sara eased off and concentrated more on developing the team. Having met the mentor and worked with him, she has also found contact with him useful.

13
Getting Mediation into Your Organization

Most procedures for dealing with conflict include a range of informal and formal steps, roughly mirroring those in Figure 7.

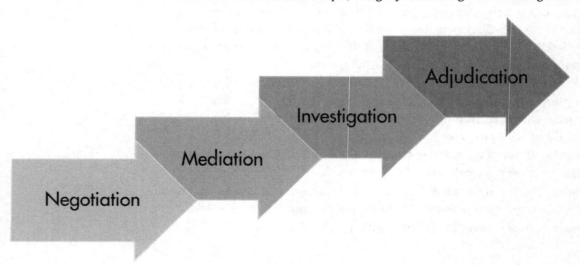

Figure 7 The range of procedures for dealing with conflict

At first people are asked to sort the conflict out themselves if they can, negotiating directly with one another. If they cannot, or do not feel sufficiently powerful, then someone, often their line manager, can act as a go-between and seek to broker an amicable solution; mediating, if you like. If this does not work, or the situation is seen as too serious to merit such an approach, some form of investigation will be conducted, and a report will be compiled covering the issues, supporting information and findings. The adjudicator(s) may seek to sort out some sort of compromise such as arbitration, or come out with a "guilty" or "not guilty" verdict. The lower down the hierarchy of options, the more directly involved the parties themselves are in the outcomes.

KEY LEARNING POINT

Each step has its merits and can work well, given the right circumstances. The trick is to promote appropriate conflict resolution, where each situation is treated on its merits and matched to the process most likely to help. Guidelines are then required to maintain people's rights and encourage constructive choices.

Mediation is most effective if introduced early into a dispute, as part of informal and formal procedures. It can also be used after an investigation, to help rebuild relationships and re-institute more effective patterns of communication.

ASSESSING THE IMPACT OF CONFLICT

People may not be too good at talking *through* conflict, but they certainly like talking *about* it. Whenever we are asked what we do for a living, in a taxi, at a party, or at a conference, the "doctor/lawyer" syndrome starts to operate. People immediately tell us about conflicts they have had themselves or witnessed. Some dramatic, painful narratives unfold and unmet needs emerge: problems they want resolved, advice they are seeking, long-held suspicions, unconfirmed or denied.

People tell us on training courses and trains alike how conflict has changed their attitude to their work: "I just do my hours, I can't be bothered, now I know it's all talk and policies; no one helped me when I was being bullied" or "My manager took us on a team-building day which was a hoot, we're not a team at all, mostly we keep to ourselves, but she doesn't seem to know what to do about it. Making towers out of toilet rolls certainly didn't improve anything." "I can't understand why no one in my department talks to one another" or "Productivity has really fallen since we employed him, it seems he has an abrasive style that the others find impossible."

These stories tell us two things:

- To speak openly about differences at work is often seen as "bad form" or "rocking the boat."
- In many cases nobody else in the workplace is listening, and nothing is done about the relentless undertone of negative conflict.

A CONFLICT AUDIT

One way of assessing the impact of conflict in an organization is to conduct a conflict audit. This works in a similar way to a stress or pressure audit, but focuses primarily on the difficulties caused by people's behavior to one another, rather than on external factors. Systems, organization, and context are considered, but only in relation to how they support negative or positive conflict.

A conflict audit should be designed to:

- **Rebuild confidence**—give people a chance to heal the damage done by costly conflict.
- **Cut the cost of conflict**—represented by time off work, demotivation, low productivity, bad decision making, poor customer or colleague relations.
- **Reinvigorate ailing groups**—remove blocks caused by the past, allow feelings to be heard, and create a focus on the future, rather than a sense of being overshadowed by the past.

A conflict audit involves several activities:

Exploration

- **Listening to conflict narratives**—setting up group and individual meetings to collect conflict narratives from key stakeholders in the organization, and to extract core issues, feelings, and views of feasible ways ahead.
- **Collecting data about conflict history**—exploring the number and type of grievances, harassment claims, bullying

incidents, tribunals, disciplinary problems, customer complaints, identifying recurring issues and what all this tells the organization.

- **Checking behavioral guidelines**—looking at practice and procedure guidelines, value statements, codes of practice or ethics, and comparing these with best practice.
- **Identifying and assessing conflict-management measures already in place**—checking grievance and harassment procedures; reviewing staff support measures to clarify the range of options in place, identify whether or not they achieve their goals, and ask whether they include a conflict-resolution capacity; assessing how equal opportunities programs address issues of conflict.
- **Organizational conflict questionnaire**—to generate data alongside the above about broad views of likely conflict hot spots, conflict-management skills deficits, and cultural factors that may contribute to negative conflict.

Levels of confidentiality need to be clearly established within a conflict audit before compiling a report. This should cover:

- **Conflict anecdotes and histories**—draw out themes and strands of people's experience of conflict, its causes and impact. Highlight case studies showing key individual, collective, and organizational issues emerging out of conflict histories. Highlight examples of negative conflict and positive ones, if there are any.

Reflection

- **Patterns**—what types of people/conflicts are involved? What passes through grievance and harassment procedures, what does not, what can be learned from them? What are the costs to the organization? Flag up risky activities, dangerous "climates" (conditions, background factors that seem to make conflict more likely), skills deficits, and process failures. Reflect on what the organization could do to learn from conflict.
- **Look to the future**—ideas for addressing key issues, including local ideas about what people want to be different. Ways of enhancing the capacity of the organization to manage conflict more effectively, including awareness raising, skill building, and providing a conflict-resolution capacity.

■ **Make projections and predictions**—assessment of the costs of conflict; reflection of the factors that sustain conflict; assessment of the costs and benefits of the conflict continuing, as against those of addressing it; assessing the feasibility of conflict transformation and the factors that can mitigate against it.

Conflict transformation

Once you have this information, the next step is to develop a conflict-management strategy, identifying proactive and reactive measures designed to prevent, manage, and resolve conflict. This could include:

■ Redesigned procedures including specific conflict-resolution measures and opportunities for early informal resolution, using practices such as mediation, prior to the conflict escalating.
■ The creation of an internal conflict-resolution capacity to provide skilled, trained specialists, who could detect conflict early, be available to help people seek resolution, and advise on what methods to use, should informal measures such as mediation fail.
■ A link-up with an external conflict-resolution service.
■ A program for training staff at all levels in conflict-management skills, mediation, assertiveness, and win/win problem solving.
■ Enhancement of support measures for staff.
■ Mechanisms to learn from conflict and draw out its positive aspects.

WHEN IS MEDIATION APPROPRIATE?

Organizations considering setting up a mediation service are well advised to ensure that people know when and how to use the service. Mediation is not appropriate for all cases, issues, or types of behavior.

Mediation works best when it is a voluntary process. Decisions should be made on each case on its merits. The following factors should be considered:

■ **The history and dynamics of the conflict**—early in the conflict is better than later.

■ **The possibility of physical threat**—it must be agreed that there is to be no violence.

■ **The nature of the relationship between disputants**—mediation is best for ongoing working relationships without unbridgeable status or rank differentials.

■ **The intensity of feeling**—if antipathy is extreme, mediation may not work.

■ **Willingness to participate in the resolution**—everyone needs to be able to contribute something.

■ **Capacity of the disputants to resolve the issues in dispute**—extreme levels of stress can leave people unable to think clearly or say what they need.

There will be the best opportunity for resolution in cases that have the characteristics in the following checklist.

CHECKLIST
CASES MOST SUITABLE FOR MEDIATION

■ Low levels of anger and physical or verbal intimidation.

■ No serious breaches of workplace guidelines.

■ No formal or other action being taken that would counter the mediation process.

■ Allegation and counter-allegation.

■ Insufficient evidence for other action.

■ Facts that are unsubstantiated.

■ Disputants who are willing to contribute to resolution.

■ Room for improvement in relationships.

■ Disputants who are not initially prepared to have face-to-face contact with their counterpart, but will with external help.

Of course, mediation is not a magic solution. It is not appropriate if:

■ There is an extreme power imbalance between the parties that cannot be bridged.

- ■ Behavior is going on between the parties that makes one or the other or both feel unsafe to negotiate.
- ■ External rules need to be applied, for example if criminal activity is involved.
- ■ One or other or both sides are unwilling or unable to mediate.
- ■ A complaint involves behavior that requires action against a perpetrator, e.g., serious misconduct, poor performance.

BUILDING MEDIATION INTO YOUR ORGANIZATION

Internationally, organizations have chosen different ways of accessing for themselves the benefits of mediation. There is no one ideal solution, as each organization has different issues to consider that will suggest certain models in preference to others. These issues include the following:

- ■ **Size**—larger organizations may need a more structured, more formal internal mediation service, because they have enough staff to enable them to work in areas other than their own, where their impartiality or independence is more visible to staff in dispute. Larger organizations will also have more staff to call on as mediators, so that their caseload won't be overly large and potentially interfere with other duties. They will also tend to have greater numbers of disputes within the workforce that call for mediation and justify the cost of running such a service. Smaller organizations might find that it is better to train one or two key staff in mediation, who can provide a solid internal resource.
- ■ **Staff turnover**—organizations with a high staff turnover may prefer to invest in training staff more broadly, rather than in training a small number in key skills, so that the skills remain in-house for longer. Conflict-management skills for managers—including an element of mediation— may be a better route, so that the general culture of the organization is changed.
- ■ **Organization culture**—organizations that already have other internal support staff, for example welfare officers,

equal opportunities officers, bullying and harassment officers, will find that developing a team of mediation officers
sits naturally within their approach to supporting their workforce. A more hierarchical organization may feel that a
senior member of staff trained to mediate fits better with
the expectations of staff and managers.

■ **Geographic spread**—a company with staff spread nation-
ally or internationally will need to consider how mediators
can work across the company generally, and how issues such
as support, standards, quality, and monitoring will be managed if there are teams of mediators in different parts of the
country.

Below we present three case studies to outline some of the different models available to organizations, and the issues to
consider.

There are three main ways of bringing mediation in house:

**BUILDING IN-HOUSE
CAPABILITY**

■ Training staff in mediation skills.
■ Developing a full in-house service.
■ Adding to the capacity of existing specialist staff.

CASE STUDY
TRAINING STAFF IN MEDIATION SKILLS

*A nationwide UK financial service institution recognized that it
had a growing number of employment tribunals, allegations of
unacceptable behavior, and a series of high-profile complaints
from trade unions about managers' incapacity to act or address
their own behavior in cases of bullying and harassment. The
director of HR and a working party set up to explore this concluded that there were a number of managerial issues left over
from a time when hierarchical systems were present and managers were expected to rule with an iron hand rather than a vel-
vet glove.*

*Mediation skills training was provided for all managers
covering:*

- *Reflective listening.*
- *Impartiality.*
- *Judgment.*
- *Win/win problem-solving skills.*
- *Defusing aggression and moving people on.*

This was aimed at shifting the culture of managing difficult situations from the coercive to the cooperative. Many of the participants were shocked that there were so many other options and their confidence grew considerably. All valued the training, particularly the way it got them to join with people in problem solving, rather than pushing others all the time.

A number of senior managers went on to complete full mediator training and found that their approach to conflict of all kinds was more creative and reflective. They were now learning from each situation, rather than moving dangerously from crisis to crisis.

CASE STUDY
ESTABLISHING A COLLEAGUE SUPPORT NETWORK

A university working group made up of a range of stakeholders, including management, union, and different staffing levels from both academic and other staff, recognized that the current grievance procedure was not doing the trick:

- *It was too adversarial.*
- *It had insufficient ways of resolving conflict built in.*
- *It had a lack of informal options.*
- *It was highly dependent on the varied skills of those who administered it.*
- *It was not contributing to building better working relationships by helping people to learn from difficult experiences.*

A different model was designed with outside help to create a five-step conflict resolution/grievance process:

1 *Informal resolution through negotiation (assisted where necessary).*

2 *Win/win problem solving.*
3 *Mediation.*
4 *Adjudication.*
5 *Appeal.*

The benefits of this model were seen to be:

■ *It builds in a number of early informal support measures to resolve grievances speedily.*
■ *It encourages conflict resolution and support at all stages.*
■ *It helps rebuild working relationships.*
■ *It gives skills to a range of staff within the organization in managing conflict wherever it arises.*
■ *It empowers people to work toward win/win outcomes.*

Initially a group of specially recruited volunteers from inside the organization were trained as a Colleague Support Network, to offer early listening support, help people to identify the best way forward, negotiate, and build up coping strategies. Recruitment and awareness-building workshops were run across the campus, followed by three days of specialized training. The university was successful in recruiting a diverse group, representing a broad variety of staff from cleaners to a dean of faculty.

Nominated members of the Colleague Support Network went on to receive full mediator training and additional staff were given investigator training, to prepare people internally to adjudicate fairly, neutrally, and thoroughly when this level of dispute resolution is called for.

CASE STUDY
BUILDING A MEDIATION CAPACITY INTO EXISTING WELFARE PROVISION

A nationwide UK government organization was already providing a high level of support for staff, with full-time welfare officers, working as a team, providing support, counseling and advice to staff within their regions. This in-house team recognized that they did not currently have a dispute-resolution capability, although they were often called on to manage situations in which conflict had happened or was about to escalate. The managers of this welfare service decided to train its team of mediators in mediation skills.

Because the team of welfare officers was highly skilled in counseling and giving advice, it was felt that they needed an interactive, people-centered approach to mediation. Four mediation programs were run in a one-week residential setting and 32 mediators trained. They now have the option of becoming accredited in practice through supervision and ongoing support and development, which offers their clients quality assurance, and a developmental path for the welfare officers.

Many of the welfare officers found the core mediation skills of impartiality, conflict resolution, and reflective listening invaluable in their own right. They were using them regularly with clients, even when the clients did not use the whole mediation process. If the early contact with a client suggested that mediation would be suitable, clear decisions had to be made about whether to continue as a mediator or a counselor. The two roles cannot be combined with one client, because there is a risk that impartiality will be lost and the welfare officer will focus only on one side of the equation.

Once welfare officers have been trained and procedural guidelines set down, it takes very little time to get a mediation service up and running, since they can receive cases through an existing network of referral points, which will be promoted through the existing mechanisms for keeping staff informed about services, and existing skill sets enable mediators to complete the training and be immediately ready for a caseload.

ACCESSING AN EXTERNAL MEDIATOR

Buying in independent, experienced mediators is the preferred option for some organizations, either on a contract basis—a certain number of cases per year, or a certain number of days per year, often resulting in a reduction in overall fees —or case by case. The benefits include:

- Access to experienced, well-trained mediators with good track records.
- Visible independence and impartiality.

- Fast interventions, normally within five days of contact with the service provider.
- Useful for senior-level disputes, where managers and directors would not feel able to use staff with less seniority as mediators.
- Expertise in difficult areas, for example group disputes or allegations of harassment, which internal mediators may lack the confidence and experience to take on.

COMBINING EXTERNAL AND INTERNAL MEDIATION SERVICES

Sometimes combining internal and external mediators can work well, provided that they are working to similar codes of practice. This can be very useful for providing mentors for newly trained mediators, for cases where people in the organization may be too well known or too senior for an internal mediator to be effective, or for those particularly complex and sensitive cases where an outside presence could have an impact.

BEST PRACTICE FOR IN-HOUSE MEDIATORS

LOCATING AND MANAGING MEDIATORS

If you are setting up a full internal mediation service, it can be tempting to go for the "agony aunts" or "born problem solvers," the counselor or most senior HR director. As should by now be clear, these people, for different reasons, may find mediation a struggle. They will also carry a resonance for potential users of their mediation service, which may put parties off doing so. When recruiting mediators it is best to use step-by-step, accessible selection methods, such as holding open information and awareness sessions, which will allow for self-selection among those who misunderstood mediation. For the staff with a more tentative approach to volunteering for things, it gives the opportunity to dip a toe in the water before committing themselves. Identify key qualities and a person specification for mediators and compare people's skills against these (see Chapter 3 for a person specification for a workplace mediator).

Ensure that selected staff's confidence matches their skills and buy in high-quality mediator training, using an accredited program. Finally, provide ongoing support and supervision on mediation practice, either within the organization or by using an external supervision provider, to ensure that they maintain suitable values and good practice.

INDEPENDENCE AND IMPARTIALITY

Internal mediation services can only too easily be seen as part of management or as a soft option. One of the main challenges facing an internal mediation service is to make explicit the boundaries around its independence. Organizations taking this route need to ensure they:

- Create a system delineating the relationship between mediation and formal methods, with clear routes in and out of the service and confidentiality guidelines.
- Offer "off-patch" mediation (where the mediator works in another organizational area and is not known to the parties) for cases where independence is difficult.
- Use mediation venues that are neutral and accessible to the workforce.
- Create publicity, stationery, and information materials that set the service apart from others provided by the organization. Avoid stereotypical images or narrow definitions of your target group, and provide translations as necessary.

EQUALITY OF OPPORTUNITY

Many people may be put off by a homogeneous mediator group. It is important when selecting mediators that they come from a broad cross-section of your workforce, and you need to give consideration to which mediators ought to take which cases. For example, a case involving sexual harassment claims may best be mediated by a man and woman working as a pair. This sends out a message of neutrality and equality. Seek guidance from specialist units, such as the Equality Officers or Racial Harassment Monitoring Units, to ensure more effective diagnosis of cases where harassment is an element, to be able to take appropriate action that fits in with your existing procedures, or work with them to redesign procedures to include early mediation.

Mediator training needs to enable mediating managers to challenge racism and other forms of oppression and discrimination as they materialize, and explore their impact on the disputants and the dispute. Finally, it is vital to monitor your track record in this area by setting up an equal opportunities monitoring group, made up of a broad representation of people from all levels of the company.

Mediation is not "justice on the cheap," a way of throwing something new at a problem and hoping that it will be sorted out without cost to the organization. The cost of having a mediation service extends beyond initial training. When using mediation other factors need to be considered:

SECURING RESOURCES

- Identify core time for mediating and build it into job descriptions for those who take on this role.
- Explore how their other activities will be covered while staff are in a mediation role.
- Take an incremental approach: pilot, followed by evaluation, and a gradual increase of caseload if effective.
- Identify a "gatekeeper" internally, a point of reference for case intake, allocation of mediators, assessment, and evaluation; build this role into their job description and offer them support and development.

Once you have set up a mediation service you will want to make sure that it is used appropriately. Organizations need to make sure that mediation is not being used only by chronic complainers, or as a way of personalizing what is, in fact, an organizational issue, for example offering one member of a team mediation where the whole team is colluding in racist behavior.

EFFECTIVE CASE INTAKE, ALLOCATION AND MANAGEMENT

To achieve effective case intake, allocation and management, you need to:

- Develop clear guidelines about which cases are most suitable for mediation and which are not, and also when to close cases.
- Build awareness of mediation, for staff and managers.
- Create case records, including details of who is involved, the nature of the dispute, details of which member of the mediation service is dealing with the case, actions taken

throughout the case, and a summary of outcomes.
- Effectively communicate about case status with all parties throughout the mediation.
- Monitor how people heard of the service.
- Allocate mediators to cases and ensure that they conduct visits within appropriate timescales.
- Take positive action to ensure that a wide variety of people can make use of the service.
- Create reporting-back procedures, including what contact the mediators have had with parties, whether agreement has been reached or not, and details of agreements reached (as determined with the parties' consent).

CHECKLIST
10 KEY FACTORS FOR A QUALITY MEDIATION SERVICE

1 Access to the service.
2 Referral, intake, and management of cases.
3 Equal opportunities.
4 Independence and impartiality.
5 Mediation practice.
6 Training, recruitment, support, and development of staff.
7 Personal safety.
8 Monitoring and evaluation.
9 Confidentiality.
10 Complaints handling.

When planning a good-quality mediation service, the following are the questions you need to answer:

ACCESS TO THE SERVICE

- How will people access mediation?
- What might prevent people from accessing the service?
- Where will the "gateway" to the service be placed?

REFERRAL, INTAKE, AND MANAGEMENT OF CASES

- What guidance, information, and skills will be required of those making referrals to the service?
- How will a consistent receipt of inquiries be managed?
- How will these inquiries get passed on to the mediation

service/the mediator?

■ How will the allocation of cases to mediators occur?

EQUAL OPPORTUNITIES

■ What specific policy statement will apply to the mediation service?

■ How will the service operate in a way that ensures no discrimination?

■ What measures will be adopted to take into account different levels of ability and special needs?

INDEPENDENCE AND IMPARTIALITY

■ What measures will the service and mediators take to ensure that they are perceived as independent and impartial?

■ What boundaries and conflicts of interest will need to be clarified and established?

MEDIATION PRACTICE

■ How will mediators maintain professional, appropriate contact with parties?

■ What administrative responsibilities will need to be completed?

■ What responsibilities will there be for continuing practice, development, support, and supervision?

TRAINING, RECRUITMENT, SUPPORT, AND DEVELOPMENT OF STAFF

■ What standards of initial and ongoing training are required?

■ What will happen if individuals do not meet or maintain this standard?

■ How have fair recruitment procedures been applied?

■ What personal support is available for mediators?

■ How will measures be taken to ensure that opportunities for development are identified and accessed fairly and equally?

PERSONAL SAFETY

■ What measures are taken to ensure that staff safety is maintained?

■ How do premises for mediation comply with personal safety requirements?

■ What type of insurance cover would need to be in place?

MONITORING AND EVALUATION

■ What information will need to be collected to evaluate the service?

- How will this information be collected, compiled, and reported?
- What measures will be taken to ensure that service improvements are made as a result of information collected through monitoring and evaluation?

CONFIDENTIALITY

- What level of confidentiality will operate within the service?
- What are the responsibilities of mediators and the service with regard to confidentiality?
- How will information on cases be recorded and stored?

COMPLAINTS HANDLING

- How will people be able to raise issues with, and complain about, the service?
- Who will deal with complaints?
- What processes will be available to resolve complaints?

EVALUATING MEDIATION

Mediating managers, fully trained independent mediators, and service coordinators or administrators need to collect data sensitively and confidentially, so that they can monitor the quality of the service and ensure that good practice is being maintained and the resources justified. Setting up comprehensive monitoring and evaluation involves:

- Keeping a record of who is using the service and how and where it is being under-used (grade, role, ethnicity, gender, part of the organization, etc.).
- Regular reports on service, including statistical analyses of cases, summaries of case status, contact of mediators with the parties, breakdowns of issues, outcomes, and other key learning points.
- Activity records detailing time spent on contact with the parties, dates, times, and duration of contacts, and administrative tasks.
- Timescales—duration of cases, response times, intervals between different stages.

■ Key issues involved in complaints—information about outcomes.

■ Information about the case-handling process—fairness, professionalism, efficiency, openness.

■ Feedback from the parties on the mediator's skills and management of the process—were the parties listened to, treated fairly and with respect; would they recommend the service to others; what was their assessment of the impact on the dispute and on their relationship?

Appendix

Materials for a Workplace Mediation Service

SAMPLE INTAKE FORM

DATE IN: . . . .

LOCATION: . . . .

Referrer/contact name: . . . .   Tel: . . . .

First mediator: . . . .   Tel: . . . .(w)
                                                                      . . . .(h)

Other contact info

Second mediator: . . . .   Tel: . . . .(w)
                                                                      . . . .(h)

Other contact info

Venue details: . . . .   Tel: . . . .

Party A contact details	Party B contact details
Brief background to case:	

PROCESS STEPS	Party A Date	Party B Date
Agreed to see mediator Attended separate sessions Agreed to face-to-face session Face-to-face session attended Feedback forms out Feedback forms in Case closed		

SAMPLE MEDIATOR'S CASE ASSESSMENT FORM

MEDIATOR'S ASSESSMENT OF OUTCOMES		MEDIATOR'S ASSESSMENT OF IMPACT	
All issues resolved		Communication improved	
Some issues resolved		Relationship improved	
No issues resolved		Some forward movement on issues	
Other		Other	

ADMIN CHECKLIST	Date done	ACTIVITY RECORD	Time taken
General information and confirmation of separate sessions sent to parties		Setting up sessions	
Parties informed about next step		Running sessions	
Information sent about groundrules		Administration	
Venue/refreshments booked		Other preparation/ activity—specify	
Agreement completed			
Agreement circulated and reviewed			
Agreement finalized			
Monitoring sheets completed			

HOW DOES MEDIATION WORK?

Mediation is a process by which an impartial, trained person helps two or more people in a dispute to talk about their situation, exchange their concerns, and come up with ideas about how to move the dispute forward. What is discussed in a mediation is confidential, and there are groundrules to help people feel confident and safe enough to communicate their needs, feelings, and concerns.

If you take part in mediation, you and the others involved in the dispute will be asked to:

- Be open about how you feel, what the problem is, and what you want.
- Listen to the other person/people.
- Think about how things could be improved in the future.
- Try to understand and accept the other people involved.

The mediator(s) will:

- Ensure that everyone has an equal opportunity to communicate (speak and listen), negotiate, and work out realistic and fair agreements.
- Prevent name calling, abuse, or behavior that prevents people from negotiating fairly.
- Not take sides or make decisions for you.

At a preliminary confidential meeting with the mediator(s) you will be able to:

- Describe the situation from your point of view.
- Think clearly about ways of moving the situation forward.
- Get to know more about how mediation works and the benefits of using mediation to find a settlement.

A confidential group meeting at which all parties are present will then be held with five stages, as follows:

Describing the problem
Each party will have a short time to open with, without interruption, to explain how they see the situation and what they would like to happen.

Exploring the issues
The mediator will ensure that people are clear what the important issues are, checking facts, comparing views of the problem, agreeing what issues can realistically be settled by mediation, and agreeing to continue.

Building agreements
The mediator will explore what people want and what can be done about the situation, working through differences, managing conflict, problem solving, and preparing for decisions.

Making agreements
The mediator will not make suggestions or tell you what to do. They will help you come up with solutions that everyone is willing to accept. They will help test likely outcomes, clarifying what will happen next, and think about what should be done if something goes wrong.

Closure and follow-up
End the session, agreeing plans for future contact between the mediator and yourselves, if necessary.

MEDIATION PARTY EVALUATION QUESTIONNAIRE

To ensure that our service is providing quality mediators, please complete and return this form to.. Your feedback will *not* be shared directly with the person who referred the case and *will* be kept strictly private and confidential.

Case no:	
Mediator(s) name(s):	

Please tick the box that best reflects your views on the following questions:

	Very	Not very	Not at all
1 How well did the mediator(s) explain what was going to happen?			
2 How well did they answer any questions you had?			
3 How well did the mediator(s) listen to you?			
4 How well were you able to express your feelings?			
5 How fairly and respectfully did the mediator(s) treat you?			
6 Did the mediator(s) allow you enough time?			
7 How well did the mediator(s) answer your questions and prepare you for the next meeting?			
8 How impartial did the mediator(s) remain?			
9 How helpful was the mediator(s) in assisting you in saying what you needed to?			
10 Did the mediator(s) pace the joint session well?			
11 Thinking back to how you felt before the mediation and how you feel now, how important was the mediator in helping you move forward?			
12 How likely are you to recommend this process to others?			
13 How acceptable were the timescales in the process to you?			

How did you hear about the mediation service?

....

Please make any further comments you may have about your experience of mediation (e.g., on the outcome or the impact of the process on your dispute).

EQUALITIES DATA—FOR MONITORING ONLY—CONFIDENTIAL INFORMATION
Please complete this section as well. Tick the boxes appropriate to you.

Male ☐   Female ☐

Age: Under 26 ☐   26–35 ☐   36–45 ☐   46–55 ☐   56–65 ☐   Over 65 ☐

Which group best describes your ethnic origin or descent?

Bangladeshi ☐   Black African ☐   Black Caribbean ☐   Black Other ☐
Chinese ☐   Indian ☐   Pakistani ☐   White ☐
Other ☐ (specify)

Sexuality: Bisexual ☐   Heterosexual ☐   Homosexual ☐   Lesbian ☐

Employment status: Employed full-time ☐   Employed part-time ☐

Do you consider you have a disability? Y / N   If yes, please describe:

Issues: In your view, what was the nature of the dispute?
Bullying   ☐   Racial harassment   ☐   Sexual harassment   ☐
Personal issue   ☐   Role allocation   ☐   Communication   ☐
Inappropriate behavior   ☐   Unfair treatment   ☐   Other (specify)   ☐

CONFLICT MANAGEMENT PLUS LTD: THE MEDIATION EXPERTS

We have provided specialist dispute resolution and conflict management training and consultancy for commercial organisations, government agencies and other public and private-sector bodies since 1989, including:

❖ Accredited mediation training
❖ Mediation and conflict management skills training for managers
❖ Investigation skills training for workplace bullying and harassment
❖ Training to encourage people from argument to dialogue

TroubleshooterUK, our dispute resolution service, also provides:

❖ **Coaching** – in conflict management skills for individuals at all levels
❖ **Mediation** – for organisations experiencing high levels of conflict in teams or between individuals at all levels
❖ **Investigation** – independent rigorous investigators
❖ **Group facilitation** – to rebuild dysfunctional teams or when a specific goal needs to be achieved; facilitating public meetings and workshops, chairing committees, providing a process and structure for multi-agency working
❖ **Neutral assessment** – independent analysis of the causes of a specific conflict and recommendations for resolution

Contact Conflict Management Plus at:

Low Farm, Brook Rd, Bassingbourn,
Royston, Hertfordshire, SG8 5NT, UK
Tel +44 (0)1763 852225
Fax +44 (0)1763 853313

Website: www.conflictmanagementplus.com
Email: info@conflictmanagementplus.com